Reflective Primary Teaching

CRITICAL
TEACHING

Reflective Primary Teaching

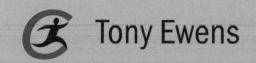

Tony Ewens

CRITICAL
TEACHING

First published in 2014 by Critical Publishing Ltd

British Library Cataloguing in Publication Data
A CIP record for this book is available from the British Library

ISBN: 978-1-909682-17-7

This book is also available in the following e-book formats:

MOBI ISBN: 978-1-909682-18-4
EPUB ISBN: 978-1-909682-19-1
Adobe e-book ISBN: 978-1-909682-20-7

Cover design by Greensplash Limited
Project Management by Out of House Publishing
Printed and bound in Great Britain by Bell and Bain, Glasgow

Critical Publishing
152 Chester Road
Northwich
CW8 4AL
www.criticalpublishing.com

Contents

Acknowledgements

I should like to thank the Lancashire and Cumbria teachers, head teachers, trainee teachers, university tutors, school governors and parents who engaged in discussion with me and granted permission for their opinions and ideas to be quoted in this book. Thanks are also due to my former colleagues and students at the University of Cumbria, staff of the Devon schools' advisory service, and teachers and pupils at the schools in Devon where I once taught, all of whom have helped to shape my views on a range of educational issues. I am grateful to Julia Morris at Critical Publishing for her incisive and helpful editorial comments, to David Campbell and the staff at Out of House Publishing for their diligence and efficiency, and to my wife, Sally, for her unfailing support and encouragement while this book was being written.

The chart in Chapter 1 is reproduced by kind permission of the CBI (The Confederation of British Industry (2012) *First Steps: A New Approach for our Schools,* London: CBI. Available online at www.cbi.org.uk/media/1845483/cbi_education_report_191112.pdf)

Meet the author

Tony Ewens worked as a teacher and head teacher in primary and middle schools in Devon, then as the county's advisory teacher for religious and moral education, before moving into Initial Teacher Education (ITE) as a lecturer at St Martin's College, now the University of Cumbria. Specialising in the philosophy of education as well as RE, he became Head of Education and Associate Dean at St Martin's College. Upon the formation of the University of Cumbria, Tony was appointed Head of Education Studies. He retired in 2008 and is now a freelance consultant, an external examiner for ITE courses and an author.

Introduction: why reflective primary practice?

This book is about becoming, and continuing to be, a successful primary school teacher. It is written in the light of the Teachers' Standards for England (Department for Education, 2011), with reference to Key Stages 1 and 2 of the English system. It is also relevant to the comparable requirements for teachers in Scotland, Wales and Northern Ireland.

What? Who? How? Why?

Good teachers constantly strive to improve their performance, by developing their knowledge of the subjects that they teach, their understanding of the pupils whom they teach and their mastery of an extended repertoire of professional skills and techniques which they use in the process of teaching. This entails hard work, not least in:

* securing a thorough knowledge of the wide range of subject matter included in the primary curriculum;

* gaining insight into the different characteristics, interests and aptitudes of a sizeable number of children; and

* acquiring a range of teaching methods and approaches, and implementing them judiciously in the context of a well-ordered classroom.

Maintaining, extending and updating each of these will be a constant feature in your work.

The teacher's role has been aptly summarised in the phrase, 'a teacher is a person who teaches someone something, somehow'. The three bulleted points above indicate the significance of each of the three: the someone, the something and the somehow.

To succeed as a teacher, you need a thorough knowledge of all three. A teacher with a good grasp of the curriculum and a sound knowledge of the pupils, but who lacks a command of a range of teaching methods is unlikely to be successful in the classroom. One who has insight into the pupils and a mastery of teaching techniques, but with inadequate subject knowledge, will teach inaccuracies and misconceptions. And a teacher with thorough knowledge of the subjects and curriculum, together with a wide array of educational approaches, but who lacks an understanding of the class, will not be able to pitch the teaching at the appropriate level for the children. You may well be able to recall teachers in these various categories, who fell short of the ideal, and also practitioners who combined all three attributes in a way that made them good or even excellent teachers.

Even a quick reading of the Teachers' Standards reveals that the trio of 'something, someone and somehow' pervades them, for example in Standard 3: *Demonstrate good subject and curriculum knowledge,* Standard 4: *Plan and teach well-structured lessons* and Standard 5: *Adapt teaching to respond to the strengths and needs of all pupils.*

These are extensive demands, calling for practitioners who can operate to a high standard across a wide range of knowledge and skills and who, by using a thoughtful, systematic approach, can be mindful of their own abilities and aptitudes and take responsibility for their ongoing professional development and progress.

In addition to all this, it is important that teachers can give answers to the question 'why?' Why are you teaching this content to those pupils in that way at this time? To say, 'because it's in the national curriculum and our school's policy requires it to be taught to my class at this time of the school year using these methods' may be true, but it is not an adequate response from a professional teacher. You need to be able to provide a rationale for the work that you do, to demonstrate your own mastery of the art and science of teaching. This requires you to be a reflective teacher, as well as a hard-working one.

Reflection and reflecting

The title of this book, *Reflective Primary Teaching*, highlights the important role that reflection plays in your formation and professional identity as a teacher. Schön (1983) and Eraut (1994) discussed in detail how members of various professions regularly use reflection as a means of analysing and improving their performance. Both wrote some time ago, but their work remains valuable for understanding professional practice. Their ideas offer you ways to build into your own work the regular use of reflective techniques so that you habitually monitor and enhance your teaching.

Schön identified a variety of ways in which professionals use reflection, including sophisticated variations such as the ability to build it into ongoing professional tasks. Eraut describes a process of 'routinisation' (Eraut, 1994) to explain why teachers and other professionals often seem to operate on 'autopilot', when aspects of their practice, on which they once reflected carefully, are subsequently repeated regularly and seemingly automatically in their daily routines. He suggests that developing a repertoire of routinised practices is a key factor in enabling professionals to deal with the multiple demands made upon them, as it reduces the number of issues requiring their conscious attention at any one time. It is, however, important that each of the routinised tasks should periodically be reviewed, by reflecting attentively on them, to check that they continue to be appropriate and effective.

In one sense, Schön and Eraut are describing a process that everyone uses regularly. Consider a conversation in which you have been involved recently. You may have reflected upon some information given to you by the person with whom you were talking and asked yourself, 'was it accurate? What is its significance? Do I need to do anything about it?' Perhaps you thought about the person's mood or motivation. Why did they say what they said? Were they worried or upset about something and did that affect their remarks? Did they have a particular agenda? Or you may have wondered about the impact that you had upon them. Did you give a positive and friendly impression or did you appear puzzled or offhand? Did you confuse or mislead them? All these are examples of an everyday situation in which we typically use reflection. You may have had these thoughts when the conversation had ended or while it was still in progress, thus highlighting Schön's distinction between 'reflection on action' and 'reflection in action'.

Apparent in this example of reflection is an approach usually described as critical analysis. When thinking about your conversation, you considered who the person was, what they said to you and why they said it. In other words, you isolated different details about the incident (analysis), then made judgements about each of the various aspects (critiquing). Notice that 'critical' is used here in the sense of making dispassionate judgements, rather than in its everyday sense of making negative comments. It is this rigorous and systematic approach to reflecting that Schön and Eraut describe in their writings, and which is commended in this book as a cornerstone of professional development and improvement.

Since reflection is a fundamental feature of our everyday life, it follows that we should be able to harness it to good effect in our professional practice as teachers. Consider these four different types of reflection that teachers commonly use:

1.   Reflecting on your own schooldays

Since you probably attended primary school for six or seven years, and secondary school for the same length of time, it is hardly surprising that your experiences as a school pupil play a major role in structuring your views about schools and education. It could hardly be otherwise. The years spent as a pupil shape your understanding of the purposes of education and your expectations of what school classrooms should be like. The same holds true for everyone else who ever attended school, including the parents of the children you teach and the politicians who frame the policies that drive the national education system. It is no wonder that we all think of ourselves as experts about schooling, since we have all – well, nearly all – undergone formal education for a long period of time.

Given the lengthy duration of your schooldays, experienced at a particularly formative time in your life, it can be difficult to conceive of any other approaches to teaching and learning than those that you encountered yourself. For that reason it is important to give some serious consideration to your experience as a school pupil. In doing so, it can be helpful to frame questions to prompt your thinking. How typical were you of the pupils in your class? What do you think were the aims that underpinned your teachers' endeavours? What did the curriculum consist of? What methods of teaching and learning were employed? Did you think that some teachers were better than others? If so, would other pupils have agreed with you? These, and many other questions, can be fruitful starting points for the practice of reflecting about your schooldays.

2. Reflecting on episodes of teaching in which you have been involved as teacher or observer

Teachers invariably think about the lesson that they have just taught, at least at the level of deciding whether it went well or badly. Reflecting analytically and critically on the lesson can help you to delve far further into what happened and why, and has the capacity to promote deep learning about your professional practice. Several considerations need to be borne in mind.

- Firstly, you do not need to adopt a deficit model of reflection. In other words, try to avoid a mindset that always looks for weaknesses and seeks ways to remedy them. While it is true that we can learn a great deal from mistakes that we make, it is also the case that we can benefit from analysing aspects of our teaching that went well. Reflecting critically on an episode in a lesson that you judged successful – the children were engaged, your explanations were understood, most pupils achieved the intended learning outcomes – may enable you to identify ways of transferring the same methods to other areas of the curriculum, or at least to plan to repeat the same approach in a future lesson. Successes can lead to further improvements. Of course, it is also true that you can learn much from analysing a disastrous lesson, particularly if you can identify what caused the problems and plan to avoid repeating the errors. But try to adopt a balanced approach, by reflecting on a mix of positive and negative features in your teaching.

- Secondly, it is not necessary always to evaluate an entire lesson when you reflect on your teaching. Reflecting in detail on just one aspect of your work may yield greater benefits. For example, you might decide to focus on how you introduced and explained to the class the main task in a science lesson. Introductions can easily become so long that the earlier instructions have been forgotten by the time the class sets to work. But too brief an instruction can skate over important points. Do you take questions from children during the explanation, with the risk that you – and they – lose the drift, or do you ask them to wait until you have finished speaking, in which case they may have forgotten what they wanted to ask? A sharply focused consideration of this part of your lesson could well have implications for your future teaching, not only in science but across the curriculum.

- Thirdly, there is much to be gained from studying your class at times when a colleague is responsible for the lesson. You may occasionally enjoy the luxury of being a neutral observer; more often you will be involved as a participant observer. For instance, you may be a trainee teacher responsible for one group of pupils in a lesson taught by the regular class teacher. You will notice things about a class under these circumstances that you would not typically observe while you are running a lesson yourself. For example, you might look closely at what is happening around one table in the room. Are all the members of the group working purposefully? Are one or two pupils doing most of the work and, if so, does it matter? Is anyone completely disengaged from the task in hand? Reflecting on your observations as an observer can prompt you to design subsequent lessons of your own in ways that address your findings. For example, when designing group work, you might build in tasks for each group member, and you might arrange for you, or a supporting adult, to ensure that a disengaged pupil participates productively.

3. Reflecting on alternative viewpoints, for example the outcomes of other people's work, and their observations or judgements

Conversation in the staffroom sometimes involves colleagues talking about the lessons that they have just taught, reporting on triumphs and disasters, and discussing them with each other. A wealth of material is available, in books, articles and magazines, which provides case studies of other people's teaching, coupled with evaluative comment by either the practitioner or someone reporting on their work. Reflecting on reports of other people's teaching can provide you with ideas to try for yourself or warn you of pitfalls to be avoided.

Just as you see things differently when observing a class being taught by a colleague, rather than by you, so you can also obtain food for thought from the comments of others who observe lessons when you are teaching. Senior fellow-teachers, such as mentors, subject leaders or head teachers, deploy their own extensive experience of teaching when watching your lesson, then offering you feedback. Because their observer status enables them to see things of which you as the teacher may be unaware, they can provide you with different perspectives. By reflecting on their input, you will often gain a broader outlook on the class, your teaching methods and the pupils' attainment than you could get solely from your own evaluations.

Feedback from inspectors and other professionals external to the school helps you to view your performance against a backdrop of a wide range of primary practice, since these colleagues have the advantage of observing teaching in a large number of schools. Although their role may principally entail giving you a grade, they will nevertheless offer some formative comments about your strengths and areas for improvement, and give advice about the next stage of your professional development. Whether their judgements delight or depress you, there is always much to be gained from reflecting on their remarks, ideally in conversation with a trusted senior colleague.

Consider, too, the value of seeking the views of other adults who know the children in your class from perspectives other than those of a teacher. Meetings with parents and carers, whether at a formal parents' evening or during an informal conversation, can be really helpful to teachers. While parents understandably want to know about their children's progress, teachers often gain insights into children's likes and dislikes, the effect upon them of particular circumstances at home and about interests they pursue outside of school. Reflecting on this information, some of which is shared with you in strict confidence, can change your understanding of some children and alter the way in which you work with them. Teaching assistants, who often work closely with small groups of children under your direction, are often in a position to offer detailed feedback about pupils' progress, misconceptions or circumstances.

Finally, but very importantly, the children themselves constantly give feedback worth noting and reflecting upon. The child who looks puzzled during your explanation, the one who sighs when you announce a maths lesson, the pupil who always seems withdrawn on Monday mornings, the one who cannot get the hang of telling the time, children who never seem to have their PE kit on the right day – all these are telling you something. If you are repeatedly looking at your lesson plan and worrying about getting through everything in time, you may well not notice these important signs, any of which might cause you to reflect and reconsider how to address an aspect of your practice.

4.   Reflecting on material that you have read

Teachers and trainee teachers have a very wide range of literature at their disposal, in web-based and printed form. Books and journals abound to support degree-level study at undergraduate, Masters and research levels and for use when seeking professional qualifications from Qualified Teacher Status (QTS) to headship. Weekly publications, such as the *Times Educational Supplement*, provide a valuable means of keeping yourself briefed on current developments and debates, and official documents from the Department for Education and other statutory bodies describe in detail the curriculum demands, assessment points and legal requirements that affect your ongoing teaching. Professional journals and magazines overflow with ideas for new approaches to a curriculum area or fresh ways of working with children. Each school also has a range of policy documents outlining agreed procedures for matters as diverse as behaviour management, reporting to parents and the conduct of educational visits.

Before reflecting on an article or a chapter that you have read, it is important to identify and appreciate the type of publication in which you have found it. For example, there are different kinds of article. Academic journals, such as the *Journal of Curriculum Studies,* contain articles submitted to an editorial board, then peer-reviewed (in other words, scrutinised by others with expertise as teachers, lecturers and researchers) before being accepted for publication. Each article will contain references to other relevant literature, demonstrate a research methodology in relation to the issue about which the author is writing and put forward an argument to support the conclusions reached by the writer. On the other hand, professional magazines, such as *Teach Primary*, contain articles offering practical advice and resources related to aspects of classroom teaching. Authors are often fellow-teachers who wish to share with a wider audience the details of a successful piece of teaching that they undertook with their class. Both types of article can be of real value to you in your work, but you probably need to read the former for your essay or dissertation and the latter when planning next week's teaching.

Critical analysis is once again the key to purposeful reflection on your reading, and as before it is best stimulated by asking questions. For example, when you read an article in an academic journal you might ask yourself whether the writer is suitably qualified and experienced to be regarded as an authority on the subject. To what extent has the author investigated the topic by reading and summarising the available literature? What methods have been used to investigate the issues? Do they appear to have been used rigorously? Do the conclusions follow logically from the evidence? Have alternative interpretations been considered? Reflecting in that way on what you read is an invaluable way to develop a judicious approach to your studying, and helps to inject balance and perspective into your essay or dissertation.

It also helps you by fostering a questioning disposition to what you read. A similar approach, used when reading professional magazines and newspapers, also helps you to increase your understanding of what happens in your classroom and to think about different approaches that can enhance your teaching.

Getting the most out of this book

Throughout the book, the four types of reflection identified above will be harnessed systematically. There is a separate chapter for each of the standards listed in Part One of the Teachers' Standards, and another for Part Two, which deals with teachers' personal and professional conduct. Since the topics covered by the chapters are not self-contained, there will be frequent cross-referencing among the chapters, to illustrate the interconnectedness of the practice of teaching.

Each chapter starts with a set of intended learning outcomes, and ends with activities labelled 'Performance of Understanding', designed to enable you to review your own achievement against the learning outcomes. Teaching is always both a practical and an intellectual activity. It is not sufficient to show that you understand how to teach reading (or whatever). You also need to demonstrate that you can do it successfully. The 'Performance of Understanding' activities are designed to prompt you to identify evidence that you both understand and can demonstrate in practice the key components of teaching set out in the Standards.

The chapters also contain reflective tasks of each of the four kinds identified above: *reflecting on your schooldays, reflecting on your teaching, reflecting on alternative viewpoints* and *reflecting on your reading*. Some of these will be stimulated by case studies drawn from typical classroom practice, some by extracts from interviews with a range of primary practitioners, and others will offer a research focus by referring you to suggested readings.

Suggestions for further reading will be made at the end of each chapter. Many of these will be from recent publications, and you are advised to keep abreast of new publications, for example by reading reviews in the educational press. Other readings are identified as 'classic texts'. These are items that date from some time ago, in some cases a very long time ago. Their purpose is twofold. On one hand they serve to show that many of the central debates in education have been in progress for ages. On the other, they offer a broader and deeper perspective than can sometimes be portrayed in a current or recent text. The politicisation of education in England, especially since the mid-1980s, means that reforms often happen in a very short period of time, to fit in with the five-year political cycle between elections. Contemporary texts are consequently at risk of being reactive to short-term events, and lose sight of broader issues and underpinning aims and theories. An acquaintance with some classic texts can help you to set your daily work and reflection against a wide backdrop, so that you can root your professional identity in firm ground.

Although written in a way which addresses the English Teachers' Standards, this book also questions their scope. Education has always been about far more than the formal curriculum, and teachers have always seen themselves as contributing to pupils' general development as persons, as well as helping them to learn subjects. As you reflect upon the Standards, you will do well to consider them in the light of your own philosophy, asking yourself, 'is there more to teaching than can be described in a set of professional standards?'

A section at the very end of this book has been left blank for your own notes and reflections.

References

Department for Education (2011) *Teachers' Standards: Guidance for School Leaders, School Staff and Governing Bodies*. DfE-00066-2011. London: The Stationery Office.

Eraut, M (1994) *Developing Professional Knowledge and Competence*. London: RoutledgeFalmer.

Schön, D (1983) *The Reflective Practitioner: How Professionals Think in Practice*. London: Temple Smith.

1 Inspiring, motivating and challenging your pupils

Learning outcomes

By the end of this chapter you should have developed and clarified:

* *an appreciation of the characteristics of a safe, stimulating and successful learning environment;*

* *an understanding of how to set goals that stretch all your pupils;*

* *an awareness of the importance of modelling the positive attitudes, values and behaviours expected of pupils.*

The first of the Teachers' Standards, 'a teacher must set high expectations which inspire, motivate and challenge pupils', should be seen as a synoptic statement. In other words, each of the other Standards makes a contribution to its achievement. Secure subject knowledge, your ability to plan good lessons and sequences of lessons, proactive use of assessment, successful behaviour management and a range of other professional attributes must be in place if you are to inspire, motivate and challenge your pupils productively.

The importance of expectation

Notice particularly that the thrust of this Standard rests upon a belief that all pupils are capable of making progress, and it requires you to believe that your pupils are no exception.

Sometimes educational theories have been thought to indicate that a pupil's capacity is finite, and that it is therefore appropriate for a teacher to have limited expectations of that child. For instance, Piaget's stage theory (Child, 2007: Section 2, Chapter 4) can be misunderstood as implying that children who are 'not ready' to move to the next stage of learning need simply to wait until they are ready. Instead, it should be seen as guiding teachers towards ways to prepare pupils for the next step. Similarly, policy debates about selective education based on intelligence testing, usefully summarised by Sumner (Sumner, 2010), have included arguments that teachers of pupils not selected for a grammar school education might lower their expectations of them. This would be difficult to establish, but a subsequent development has seen Ofsted paying close attention to grammar schools. It has been suggested (Davis, 2012) that some grammar schools have 'coasted', because of assumptions that their pupils will do well regardless of the efforts of their teachers. Both examples illustrate how teachers' perceptions of pupils' potential for educational achievement can be shaped by misconception and misunderstanding.

Teachers' expectations of pupils

There is plenty of evidence that high expectations lead to an improvement in performance. It is also true that teachers' expectations of children need to be realistic, otherwise they may be setting up their pupils to fail (Stewart and Harris, 2007). Three examples from psychology, the Hawthorne effect, the Pygmalion effect and the Halo effect, are especially relevant to teaching.

The Hawthorne effect (summarised by Hindle, 2008) is named after a study in the 1920s at the Hawthorne Works, an electric plant in Illinois, which demonstrated that workers' output improved when they knew they were being studied, but fell after the experiment ended. The experimenters concluded that the workforce had responded positively to the interest being shown in their performance. The gains in productivity were due to a change in attitudes and owed nothing to increases in skills or knowledge.

The Pygmalion effect, named from George Bernard Shaw's novel, stems from a study by Rosenthal and Jacobson (1968), who told a group of elementary school teachers that particular children in their classes could be identified, from a set of standardised test scores, as 'late bloomers', who could be expected to show a spurt in their progress. In fact, the named children had been chosen at random and there was no evidence that their potential was any different from that of their classmates. However, these children made greater progress than the other pupils, demonstrating that when teachers expect children to do well, they tend to do so.

The Halo effect was first noted by the behavioural psychologist Thorndike, and refers to people's tendency to make generalised judgements about others. Rather than seeing others in mixed terms, we are inclined to regard them positively or negatively across the board, often based on initial or superficial impressions. For example, Nisbett and Wilson (1977) showed that people's impressions of the subject of a taped interview were strongly influenced by the interviewee's demeanour, rather than the content of his replies.

These three phenomena hold significant implications for teachers, some of which are identified in the following reflective task.

REFLECTIVE TASK

Reflecting on alternative viewpoints

Read these comments from a number of experienced teachers, who were asked the question, 'from your experience of teaching, what advice would you give to recently qualified teachers about the expectations they should have of pupils?' What conclusions do you draw from their responses?

- It's important to be aware of children's dates of birth. In any year group there will be a gap of almost 12 months between the oldest (September birthdays) and youngest (August birthdays), and this represents a substantial difference in sheer experience of life, including physical growth, language development, emotional maturity and general resilience, especially in infant classes. Expectations therefore need to be framed with individuals in mind.

- That issue is further highlighted if you have a mixed-age class.

- Don't assume that children for whom English is not the first language used at home are less capable than other pupils. Bilingualism can be a great asset.

- It is wrong to assume that younger siblings of children who have already passed through the school will have the same interests and aptitudes as their brothers or sisters.

- I realised a few years ago that I tended to expect more from children who were taller than their peers, but that's quite irrational.

- Beware of any tendency to write off children who are badly behaved. Naughtiness doesn't imply a lack of ability. Sometimes it's linked with issues that are totally divorced from school and learning, and sometimes it can even be a sign that a child isn't being sufficiently challenged at school.

- Make sure that you assess children objectively. You can easily find that you downgrade pupils who give you grief by their behaviour and overestimate the capability of beautifully behaved ones.

- Children who are quiet or shy can easily be underestimated and too little may be expected of them.

- Don't assume that children who are neatly dressed and well-spoken are cleverer than their classmates.

- Don't assume that a child who is good at one area of the curriculum will necessarily be good at another.

- When I taught a child with cystic fibrosis, and another with spina bifida, I came to realise that, because of their physical limitations, both tended to spend quite a lot of their free time in activities that engaged their brains and gave them lots of incidental *practice in language and number. Both could consequently respond to a high level of challenge from me, and I learned to raise my expectations of them.*

- *Your knowledge of parents' social status or occupation, or the type of house they live in, should not play any part in framing your expectation of their children's potential.*

- *If you sense that there is not much educational aspiration coming from a child's family, don't sit in the staff room blaming the parents. Redouble your efforts to show pupils the benefits of education and to convince them that they can do it.*

- *Half the battle is getting pupils to believe that they can achieve. You have to make it clear that you believe in them, give them tasks that will stretch them, support them with encouragement and praise, and recognise their achievements.*

- *There's no such word as 'can't', and your job as a teacher is to work out 'how'. If children don't understand something, that's your problem, not theirs, so don't blame them. Find a new way of explaining the concept.*

- *You need two types of relationship with your class, one that you use to control the whole group, and another that is a series of one-to-one relationships with each of the individual children. You need to know their different circumstances – personal as well as educational – and match your strategies to their needs.*

The teachers quoted above responded very readily to the question and could clearly relate the topic to specific circumstances that they had encountered in their classrooms. Studying their responses in the light of the Hawthorne, Pygmalion and Halo effects, the following key points emerge:

- The Hawthorne effect implies that children's attitudes to their work will be positively influenced if they know that the teacher and other staff are actively interested in, and accurately informed about, their progress. Generating good attitudes towards tasks is likely to enhance outcomes irrespective of formal teaching and learning. A demanding, yet realistic, expectation from you should be supported by active monitoring of pupils' performance. Feedback, while offering encouragement, should not be uncritical; in other words, you need to balance praise with challenge. This implies that you know each of your pupils, and their previous achievement, well enough to set your expectations at a level which will stretch them without overloading them.

- The Pygmalion effect should prompt you to work on the assumption that there will be improvement on the part of each child. In particular you should be scrupulous in ensuring that you do not reduce your expectation because of a child's social or ethnic background, gender, height, size or conduct. Matching the level of challenge to the individual children in the class is dependent on having an accurate picture of what they already know and can do. Different types of expectation apply according to circumstance. For example, your expectations of the whole class ought to relate to general matters, such as making a wholehearted effort. When considering individual pupils, you need to differentiate what you expect in terms of specific outcomes, based on your knowledge of their prior achievement. This should inform your decisions about the progress that you expect individual pupils to make.

- The Halo effect ought to draw your attention to the importance of looking carefully and objectively at different aspects of a child's performance, rather than classifying pupils as generally 'good' or 'poor'. Using profiling (see Chapter 6) as an assessment tool can help you to chart a pupil's differential performance across the areas of the curriculum, and indeed across different aspects within a subject. It is also important to ensure that your judgements about a child's performance are not coloured by initial impressions. For example, subjective marking tends to reward good behaviour and neat presentation rather than focusing rigorously on the knowledge and skills being assessed. You need therefore to use objective criteria, related to intended learning outcomes, when assessing children's work.

The first teacher quoted above stressed the importance of framing expectations with individuals in mind, and the last asserted the desirability of having two types of relationship with your pupils, one with the class as a whole, the other an individual rapport. The requirement to match your level of expectation to the developmental circumstances of individual pupils is extremely demanding, and will often elude thorough achievement. Setting out your expectations for a class as a whole is necessarily a far more approximate exercise, but it is easier and you should not undervalue its importance. A key lesson from the Hawthorne effect is that positive attitudes tend to lead to improved performance, irrespective of formal teaching and learning. Consequently, being in a stimulating classroom, and belonging to a class which is responsive to the values and culture that its teacher fosters, can be a springboard enabling each class member to leap forward.

Swann et al. (2012) analysed developments at one school based on a reappraisal of learning in a stimulating environment informed by a belief that each child's potential for learning is limitless.

Expectation, aspiration and society

You will rightly be concerned first and foremost with what you should expect of your own class in the current school year. However, it is also valuable to stand back and reflect on wider contexts. If you accept that an important role of education is to help children to prepare for adult life, including employment opportunities, you need to consider what life might be like for your pupils in 20, 40 or 60 years' time. The rate of social and economic change in the past 20 years has been immense. One measure of this is the fact that computers only became important in primary schools in the 1990s. Given the rate of change stimulated by technological developments, you can only speculate on the shape of the future. Yet as a teacher you share responsibility for preparing children to play their part in it, so that they can lead fulfilling lives. This has massive implications for how you define the goals of education.

REFLECTIVE TASK

Reflecting on your reading

CBI (The Confederation of British Industry) (2012) *First Steps: A New Approach for Our Schools*. London: CBI.

In 2012 the CBI commenced an education campaign, initiating a debate about the sort of educational outcomes that employers believe are needed if today's children are to play a full part in the workplace, and the wider society, of the future. 'First Steps' is a report based on discussions with employers, teachers and academics. Read the executive summary (pages 6 to 9), noting particularly the references to primary education. Notice, too, the emphasis the employers place on the balance between core knowledge and holistic personal development, both of which they regard as crucial. Read, too, the report's commendation of the Singapore education system's Desired Outcomes of Education (DOE) statement (exhibit 14 on p 28).

» *Do the report's key findings reflect your experience as a primary school teacher?*

» *To what extent do you agree with the report's recommendations?*

» *How do you respond to the assertion that Singapore's success in building a world-class education system is associated with a reduction in the amount of subject matter taught and an increase in the learning of life-long skills, the building of character and competencies such as critical thinking and creativity (p 28)?*

Economic and technological changes have rapidly affected the types of employment available in England. Industries previously reliant on large numbers of unskilled staff have either been outsourced to countries with cheaper labour costs or been transformed through mechanical and technological innovation so that a radically different labour force is required. Some of these industries were geographically concentrated, for example shipbuilding, car manufacturing, textiles, steelmaking and coal mining, many of which traditionally provided largely male employment, and this means that there are parts of the country still coming to terms with a revolutionary change in the nature of opportunities for work. Other occupations, notably agriculture, are spread around the country, but changes in the labour force have been just as severe. The log book of one rural Devon school records that in the 1930s 38 parents were employed as agricultural workers. By 1987 this figure had dropped to one. Against this sort of backdrop it is unsurprising that many parents are bewildered about their children's prospects and uncertain about the sorts of aspirations they might have for their educational outcomes.

It is in the light of these stark changes, especially though not exclusively for male employment, that the CBI report should be read. Employers not only emphasise that pupils need to leave school with good core knowledge in language, mathematics, science and computer science, but also that 'there is a set of behaviours and attitudes, a kind of social literacy that we should foster' (CBI, 2012, p 31). The CBI report identifies a set of 'characteristics, values and habits that last a lifetime' (CBI, 2012, p 33) and argues that the formation of character should sit alongside academic achievement as central to the work of schools. It also asserts that gaining the involvement of parents and communities is fundamental to schools' success.

REFLECTIVE TASK

Reflecting on your teaching

With reference to a half term of recent teaching, identify examples of how your work helped children to develop and extend some of the qualities set out in Exhibit 19 on p 33 of the CBI report.

Pring's (1996) chapter on values and education policy provides an insightful discussion of ways of overcoming the seeming divide between academic and vocational approaches to the curriculum. He offers useful suggestions about integrating practical and theoretical knowledge, in a context which takes seriously the notion of 'social literacy' advocated by the CBI. Pring also makes a case for retaining the notion of a liberal education, defined as 'learning for its own sake', in which knowledge is pursued as being intrinsically of interest and worth. He argues that it is beneficial for society if schools help their pupils to develop their own academic interests and enthusiasms. While acknowledging the important instrumental purposes of education as preparation for adult life, Pring concludes that schooling need not be divided between academic and vocational pathways. His description of a 'vocationalised' education seeks to incorporate both strands.

A safe and stimulating environment

The Hay/McBer organisation was commissioned by the then government to undertake research into teacher effectiveness. It found that the type of classroom created by a teacher was an important component of teacher effectiveness.

REFLECTIVE TASKS

Reflecting on your reading

Hay/McBer Group (2000) *Research into Teacher Effectiveness: A Model of Teacher Effectiveness*. (DfEE Research Report 216). London: DfEE.

The Hay/McBer report found that teachers' effectiveness was related not only to their professional characteristics (values, commitments and attitudes) and their teaching skills, but also to the classroom climate that they fostered. They defined classroom climate as 'the collective perceptions of pupils about what it feels like to be a pupil in any particular teacher's classroom, where these perceptions influence every student's motivation to learn and perform to the best of his or her ability' (Hay/McBer, 2000, 1.4.1, p 27).

Skim-read the Hay/McBer report, then focus on the sections dealing with teachers' professional characteristics.

» *Can you relate their findings to teachers who taught you, or even to your own characteristics?*

The Hay/McBer team interviewed a significant number of pupils across the age range, and found that they preferred teachers who were firm but fair, friendly but not over-familiar, well organised, good at explaining and patient with pupils who found the work difficult.

» *Would you have agreed with this when you were at primary school?*

Reflecting on your schooldays

Thinking about your time at primary school, try to identify a teacher whom you admired and respected. Think particularly about the classroom climate that they promoted.

» *What was it like to be in their class?*

» *How did they succeed in helping you to learn?*

» *How did they maintain an orderly environment?*

» *What personal qualities impressed you?*

» *What can you learn from that teacher about the sort of teacher you would like to become?*

Eaude (2012) draws attention to the value of knowing about your pupils' backgrounds. His claim that 'teachers with a high level of expertise search out, show respect for, and draw on, the knowledge and interests of all children, especially those who may be reluctant to share these' (Eaude, 2012, p 51) is supported by reference to his own teaching. He found that children were more animated when asked about their own culture, religion or interests, and that many became much more engaged when given practical tasks associated with what they understood from experience outside of school. Your classroom is more likely to be a safe and stimulating place for your pupils if your planning reflects your knowledge of them, as well as your knowledge of the school's curriculum.

A safe classroom

The idea of safeguarding ought to be seen positively, since it is primarily about promoting children's welfare. One aspect of this is fostering children's resilience, since by enhancing their confidence and knowledge teachers can reduce pupils' vulnerability to some potential hazards. This does not entail seeking to eliminate all risks from the classroom. Indeed, giving children opportunities to deal with risks in a secure and supportive setting is an important way to enhance their resilience. Creating a positive relationship between you and your class is a central factor.

REFLECTIVE TASK

Reflecting on your reading

Macpherson (2011, p 137) depicts an ideal classroom as one that exhibits an appropriate emotional climate, as well as a productive learning environment, since this provides a counterbalance to children's lack of power, a feature that makes them especially vulnerable.

» *Read this section of Macpherson's chapter, and consider her claim that the trust built between pupil and teacher in an emotionally mature classroom is key to developing their security and resilience.*

» *What factors do you think are likely to help you to build such a relationship with your classes?*

The formal curriculum can also be an effective vehicle for building resilience. Teaching about the safe use of online communications, how to eat healthily and keep fit, and how to use equipment and apparatus safely are obvious examples, all of which are made more effective if put into practice as well as spoken about. Learning approaches can also contribute. For example, structured work in small groups can enable some children to voice their opinions and ideas whereas they might be apprehensive about speaking to the whole class.

REFLECTIVE TASK

Reflecting on your teaching

» *Thinking about a class in which you work or have previously worked, identify any aspects of the curriculum which helped you to promote children's resilience, whether by means of the subject matter that they studied, the skills that they practised or the ways in which they learned.*

» *Was this the result of deliberate planning, or something that you can only see with hindsight?*

» *Where else in the curriculum might you find potential for this sort of outcome?*

In general, safeguarding is associated with the thoughtful implementation of good professional practices.

Promoting children's well-being includes measures such as ensuring that your classroom contains no obvious physical hazards, monitoring procedures for moving safely around the school and giving clear directions for the use of apparatus in, for instance, technology and PE. Particular care is needed when planning to take children away from the school premises. Schools have policies and protocols for educational visits, designed to enable teachers to anticipate and avoid problems, and these are directed by an Educational Visits Co-ordinator (EVC). You will need to liaise with this colleague before planning such activities.

As well as adopting good practices you need actively to avoid poor practice, not least because it might give rise to suspicions or allegations against you. Some issues are clear cut; for example, sanctions involving physical punishment are prohibited. Other areas are greyer. Some people suggest that teachers should avoid touching children, while others maintain that offering comfort to a distressed child or restraining an aggressive one are integral to a teacher's professional duty. As a teacher, you have easy access to children, you are present when they are changing clothes or undressing, for swimming for example, and you can sometimes be alone with a child. Your personal conduct at these times must be beyond reproach. You are best advised to follow Macpherson's maxim that 'good practice means operating in an atmosphere of transparency so that no one questions your motives or actions' (Macpherson, 2011, p 145).

This section has dealt with safeguarding as a broad concept. 'Child Protection' is a particular instance of safeguarding referring to the activity undertaken to protect specific children who are suffering, or are likely to suffer, significant harm. This category is dealt with in detail in Chapter 9.

A stimulating classroom

Hay/McBer found that 'outstanding teachers create an excellent classroom climate and achieve superior pupil progress largely by displaying more professional characteristics at higher levels of sophistication within a very structured learning environment' (Hay/McBer, 2000, 1.1.9, p 9). When researchers questioned children about the type of classroom climate that they preferred, pupils mentioned a variety of factors. Some related to safety, for example expecting teachers to maintain order and discipline. However, many reflected a desire to learn in a stimulating environment, which pupils typically defined as having opportunities to participate actively in the class and for it to be an interesting and exciting place.

REFLECTIVE TASKS

Reflecting on your teaching

»   *With reference to your recent teaching, reflect on the extent to which your classroom has the 'Climate Dimensions' set out in Hay/McBer (2000), Section 1.4.3 (p 27f). Identify your current strengths in this area and think about how you might extend them to other aspects of your work.*

Reflecting on your schooldays

»   *Identify some examples from your own education in which you recognise that you were working in a stimulating classroom.*

»   *What characteristics of the teacher's practice created this sort of learning environment?*

Among the factors that you ought to consider in your own classroom are its layout and the use that you make of displays. Galton et al. (1999) discuss the correlation between classroom layout and teaching styles. It might seem obvious that discussion in groups can be facilitated by seating children in small groups around tables, or that copying examples from a whiteboard is easier if pupils are facing the board. Yet teachers do not always re-arrange furniture to suit the purpose of the tasks that they have planned. Nor do their lessons necessarily match their declared purposes. For example, activities designed as 'group tasks' are sometimes individual tasks being tackled by children who happen to be sitting round a table. If the classroom is large enough, an obvious plan is to arrange different areas for different types of learning: one with seats facing forward where adult input is central; another set up for structured play; one for groupwork; one where individual pupils can work unhindered at a table, easel or computer.

REFLECTIVE TASK

Reflecting on alternative viewpoints

Read this extract from an external examiner's feedback to a trainee teacher following observation of a lesson in which Year 6 pupils had been asked to write some poetry following exposure to a beautifully prepared and presented stimulus:

I was delighted that you had written a poem about the same theme before the lesson, and that you shared your work with the class. However, I sense that you were disappointed with their efforts. Could that have had something to do with the fact that they were sitting in groups around tables, discussing what they were doing? I'm sure that, when you wrote your piece, you were sitting on your own with no-one to distract you. The content of your lesson was very good, and you presented it in a very stimulating way. Next time, could I suggest that you let the children space out around the room – and beyond, into the corridor if possible – when it's their turn to write, because this sort of writing is about a personal and individual response.

» *To what extent do you consider classroom layout and use of space when planning for a stimulating learning environment?*

Smawfield (2006) offers excellent advice on displays for classrooms and beyond, in terms of both techniques of presentation and, more significantly, educational purposes. Initial interest in a topic may be engendered by one display, while another may provide an input of informative material, a third may offer a bank of related vocabulary, a fourth may provide directions for undertaking a skills-based task and a fifth may grow as a result of children's contributions being added to it. Well-designed displays are not there primarily to decorate the room, but to support and enrich a broad, varied and relevant curriculum.

REFLECTIVE TASK

Reflecting on your reading

Marshall, S (1963) *An Experiment in Education*. Cambridge: Cambridge University Press.

Dip into this classic text for an insight into how a remarkable teacher – she ran a one-teacher school for the entire primary age range in a village – created a very stimulating classroom. Notice how rigorous teacher-led input was complemented by opportunities for children to make their own responses to the material. Marshall was neither just traditional, nor just progressive – she was both. Her classroom was teacher centred and child centred at the same time.

In summary, a stimulating classroom is one in which children encounter challenges designed to promote their spiritual, moral, mental and physical development as individuals and as members of the class. The goal of keeping pupils interested should not be confused with the notion of keeping them entertained. Teachers can all too easily work incredibly hard to provide lessons which entertain children while teaching them little. Techniques that gain and maintain children's interest are invaluable, but should be used in contexts which engage them in demanding and worthwhile learning, and which help them to achieve challenging goals.

Setting goals that challenge pupils

In order to know what will challenge pupils, you obviously need to know what they already know, understand and can do. As with any form of assessment, gauging children's prior learning is a complex matter and this is dealt with fully in Chapter 6. If you are taking over a class at the beginning of a school year, you will have access to records from the previous year. There may be some issues about the validity and/or reliability of the assessment tools used. If some pupils are joining you from other schools there may be a delay in receiving their records. You also need to bear in mind that some ground may have been lost, at least temporarily, during the long summer holiday. Initial activities with the class, including carefully chosen questions distributed around the room, as well as written and practical tasks, should therefore be designed to help you to confirm or adjust earlier assessment data.

Having made initial judgements, which you should regard as provisional, the way forward is a matter of taking careful note of children's engagement in, and response to, the tasks that you set, then acting on your findings. Eaude aptly remarks that teachers need a wide spectrum of knowledge, including propositional and procedural knowledge (knowing what and knowing how) and also personal and interpersonal knowledge (Eaude, 2012, p 11). In order to be successful in matching tasks to learners, you need to employ all these types of knowledge simultaneously. Selecting appropriate content to help pupils to move forward is not only a question about your subject knowledge. It also makes demands upon your knowledge of the children, their interests and prior experiences, and their general skills as well as their specific knowledge of the subject in hand.

REFLECTIVE TASK

Reflecting on alternative viewpoints

Experienced teachers were asked to identify cases in which they had successfully moved children forward with challenging goals, and others in which they had been unsuccessful. These extracts represent one of each type.

» *Consider the points that the teachers made. Can you relate them to your teaching experience?*

Teacher A: *Years ago, in my first year of teaching, with a Year 3 class, the head challenged me to get Tom reading. He had made little progress to date, and his reading age on the test used at our school was about 18 months below his chronological age. I naïvely set a target of getting him up to chronological age by the end of the year. Things started badly. Then, by chance, I found out that Tom was fascinated by military history and had a large collection of model soldiers. We abandoned the reading scheme and instead Tom and I composed whole books of stories about military events. He enjoyed reading these at school and at home, and that was a turning point. After that, his progress was amazing and he exceeded my target soon after Easter.*

Teacher B: *We had a small group of children who were making no progress in maths. Our well-regarded maths scheme produced a new book especially designed for pupils who were struggling. The topics were broken down into smaller, easier stages, but the format did not look in the least patronising – which is sometimes an issue. We eagerly sent for some copies. But it didn't make any difference, and we abandoned them. Later we learned that the reading level required to use the book was harder than that for the main scheme.*

Targets and levels

Previously the attainment levels associated with the national curriculum in England have been used by the government and Ofsted in ways which have turned them into targets for pupils' achievement at certain ages. For example, Level 2 and Level 4 have been identified as the expected levels of attainment by the end of Year 2 and Year 6 respectively. Moreover, the government's floor target, that 60 per cent of pupils in Year 6 in every school should attain Level 4 in English and mathematics, gave special prominence to that level as a target.

This approach to target setting has been widely criticised, including in the CBI report. On the one hand, the floor target implies that it is acceptable that 40 per cent of children leaving primary school should be behind the expected level, and it says nothing about the differential attainment of those who have met the target (some of whom may have reached Level 5, for example). Thus there is a concentration on those who are 'average'. On the other hand, by focusing narrowly on academic achievement in two subjects, the floor target draws attention away from the fact that other outcomes of education, especially those connected with character and personal development, are also vital to society in general and the future economy in particular (CBI, 2012, p 6).

A close examination of the system of grading by levels shows it to be imprecise and relatively uninformative. For instance, the fact that the four years of Key Stage 2 education have been represented by two levels of expected progress implies that each level is worth two years of schooling. Yet two children, separated by just one mark in their Key Stage 2 SAT, may have been allocated different levels, suggesting that one is two years behind the other, even though their achievements are almost identical. The division of levels into sub-levels a, b and c at each level, while marginally more informative, still produces a system in which each sub-level represents about eight months of progress. When taken together with the fact that the children thus assessed may differ in age by virtually a whole year, the imprecision of the system reveals it to be unfit for purpose.

In the light of the many criticisms of attainment levels, the government decided to abandon them at the time of the introduction of the new national curriculum in September 2014. Steps are currently being taken to supersede the levels-based approach, while retaining an emphasis on measuring progress. The issues associated with the debate about an appropriate model of assessment and target setting are further discussed in Chapter 6.

Taking seriously the comments of the CBI, you may find it helpful to focus on the achievements of each individual child, rather than the average outcomes of the whole class or year group. This would mean ensuring that initial assessments are accurate in September, then expecting a specific amount of progress as a minimum during the year. Under the outgoing system, a figure of two sub-levels for each child would be suitably challenging. Notice how this approach steers away from the notion of the average pupil. It implies that every child is expected to make progress, but from their real starting points. Thus a pupil in Year 3 who starts the year at Level 1b in English and Level 3a in mathematics will be expected to reach Level 2a in English and Level 3c in mathematics by the end of the school year. No pupils get 'written off' because they have no hope of reaching their expected targets, and no pupils are allowed to coast because they have already exceeded them. Consequently, you show respect to all your pupils, by honouring achievement at whatever level. You also avoid the dangers of the Halo effect, because you are realistic about attainment subject by subject.

But notice that this approach, pertinent as it may be to measuring academic progress, remains silent about the behaviours and attitudes comprising what the CBI termed 'social literacy'.

Modelling the attitudes, values and behaviours that you expect of pupils

Pupils are quick to identify their teachers' dispositions and preferences, and this topic is further developed in Chapter 5 when considering the hidden curriculum. It is important to be aware of your own beliefs and ideas, and to take steps to overcome undue bias in the views and attitudes that you portray. Pupils dislike any display of favouritism or preferential treatment of any child or group. You should also take care not to show personal antipathy towards any area of the curriculum. Children respond to the environment in which they find themselves. You can valuably audit the extent to which you consciously promote and model the qualities and characteristics that you expect of your class, since it is these that should feature prominently in forming the classroom environment. A helpful audit tool is suggested in the following reflective task.

REFLECTIVE TASK

Reflecting on your teaching

Consider the following chart (continued overleaf), which is reproduced by kind permission of the CBI (CBI, 2012, p 33).

Exhibit 19 Characteristics, values and habits that last a lifetime

The system should encourage young people to be	This means helping to instil the following attributes	Pupils will, for example:
Determined	Grit, resilience, tenacity	• Finish tasks started and understand the value of work • Learn to take positives from failure experienced • Work independently and be solutions focused
	Self-control	• Pay attention and resist distractions • Remember and follow directions • Get to work right away rather than procrastinating • Remain calm even when criticised • Allow others to speak without interruption
	Curiosity	• Be eager to explore new things • Ask and answer questions to deepen understanding
Optimistic	Enthusiasm and zest	• Actively participate • Show enthusiasm • Invigorate others
	Gratitude	• Recognise and show appreciation for others • Recognise and show appreciation for their own opportunities
	Confidence and ambition	• Be willing to try new experiences and meet new people • Pursue dreams and goals
	Creativity	• Identify and develop new ideas

The system should encourage young people to be	This means helping to instil the following attributes	Pupils will, for example:
Emotionally intelligent	Humility	• Find solutions during conflicts with others
	Respect and good manners	• Demonstrate respect for feelings of others • Know when and how to include others • Be polite to adults and peers
	Sensitivity to global concerns	• Be aware of pressing global issues, and contribute to leading society internationally

» *Use the chart as the basis for conducting an audit of the qualities that you promote in the classroom. Using their list of attributes (grit, resilience, tenacity, etc.) identify examples of ways in which you have succeeded in modelling them for your class.*

» *Find the areas in which you consider yourself have been most successful.*

» *Reflect on ways of tackling areas in which you decide you ought to develop your practice, and make plans to incorporate them into your subsequent planning.*

Performance of understanding

Thinking about the school in which you work or have recently worked, respond to the prompts after each intended learning outcome, as a means of identifying your knowledge and understanding of the issues covered in the chapter.

• *an appreciation of the characteristics of a safe, stimulating and successful learning environment;*

  – Identify the steps that you take to ensure that children are safe, physically and emotionally, in your classroom, and that they feel safe.

  – Explain how a visitor to your classroom would recognise it as a stimulating learning environment.

  – Articulate what you mean by a successful learning environment. How do you know when learning has been successful?

• *an understanding of how to set goals that stretch all your pupils;*

  – Demonstrate, by means of two or three examples, how you differentiate your planning and teaching to ensure that children are stretched by the challenges that you present in their lessons.

- In what ways can you involve children in setting appropriate and challenging goals for themselves, and in measuring their progress towards achieving them?

- *an awareness of the importance of modelling the positive attitudes, values and behaviours expected of pupils.*

  - In what ways are your pupils aware of your expectations of them in terms of effort, behaviour and outcomes? How important is it to state these overtly?

  - Give two or three examples which show that you sometimes undertake learning tasks alongside your pupils.

  - Explain what you mean by a teacher showing respect to his or her pupils. How would your class recognise this in your professional conduct?

  - What steps do you take to ensure that teaching assistants and other adults working with you share and model the values that you are trying to foster?

Taking it further

CBI (The Confederation of British Industry) (2012) *First Steps: A New Approach for Our Schools*. London: CBI.

Swann, M, Peacock, A, Hart, S and Drummond, M J (2012) *Creating Learning without Limits*. Maidenhead: Open University Press.

References

CBI (The Confederation of British Industry) (2012) *First Steps: A New Approach for Our Schools*. London: CBI. Available online at www.cbi.org.uk/media/1845483/cbi-education-report-191112.pdf (accessed 6 January 2014).

Child, D (ed) (2007) *Psychology and the Teacher*. Eighth edition. London: Continuum.

Davis, A (2012) 'Coasting Grammars' under Fire from Schools' Guide. *The Evening Standard,* 10 May 2012.

Eaude, T (2012) *How Do Expert Primary Class Teachers Really Work?* Northwich: Critical Publishing.

Galton, M, Hargreaves, L, Comber, C, Wall, D and Pell, A (1999) *Inside the Primary Classroom: 20 Years On*. London: Routledge.

Hay/McBer Group (2000) *Research into Teacher Effectiveness: A Model of Teacher Effectiveness*. (DfEE Research Report 216). London: DfEE.

Hindle, T (2008) The Hawthorne Effect. *The Economist,* 3 November 2008.

Macpherson, P (2011) Safeguarding Children, in Hansen, A (ed) *Primary Professional Studies*. Exeter: Learning Matters.

Marshall, S (1963) *An Experiment in Education*. Cambridge: Cambridge University Press.

Nisbett, R and Wilson, T (1977) The Halo Effect: Evidence for Unconscious Alteration of Judgements, *Journal of Personality and Social Psychology*, 35 (4): 250–56.

Pring, R (1996) Values and Education Policy, in Halstead, J M and Taylor, M J (eds) *Values in Education and Education in Values*. London: Falmer Press.

Rosenthal, R and Jacobson, L (1968) *Pygmalion in the Classroom: Teachers' Expectations and Pupils' Intellectual Development*. New York: Rineholt and Winston.

Smawfield, D (2006) Classroom and School Display. Available online at www.davidsmawfield.com/assets/img/classroom-display-handbook.pdf (accessed 5 January 2014).

Stewart, D and Harris, T (2007) Entitlement and Potential: Overcoming Barriers to Achievement, in Zwozdiak-Myers, P (ed) *Childhood and Youth Studies*. Exeter: Learning Matters.

Sumner, C (2010) 1945–1965: The Long Road to Circular 10/65, *Reflecting Education*, 6 (1): 90–102.

Swann, M, Peacock, A, Hart, S and Drummond, M J (2012) *Creating Learning without Limits*. Maidenhead: Open University Press.

2 Promoting children's learning

Learning outcomes

By the end of this chapter you should have developed and clarified:

- *an appreciation of a teacher's accountability for children's learning;*

- *a knowledge of how a range of theories of learning can help you to plan, conduct and evaluate your work;*

- *an understanding of the importance of matching your teaching plans to pupils' capabilities and prior knowledge; and*

- *an awareness of techniques for involving children in understanding, monitoring and evaluating their own work.*

You will not be surprised that responsibility for promoting children's learning is central to the Teachers' Standards. Arguably, the requirement set out in Standard 2, 'Promote good progress and outcomes by pupils', is the key task of a teacher, and the other Standards can be viewed as important means to this principal end.

Accountability

The first exemplification statement under Standard 2 makes it clear that teachers are accountable for the attainment, progress and outcomes of their pupils. Levitt et al. (2008) describe accountability as an ethical concept which deals with the responsibilities of individuals and organisations for their actions towards other people and agencies. They quote with approval Bovens' (2005) definition of accountability as 'a social relation in which an actor feels an obligation to explain and to justify his or her conduct to some significant other' (p 2). In a wide-ranging literature review, Levitt et al. identify pressures placed upon teachers by an increasing emphasis on accountability. They suggest particularly that a risk may be posed to teachers' professionalism if they are required to respond to a growing range of external demands, which may be perceived as limiting the scope of professional judgement. Before analysing their conclusions, it is valuable to consider to whom you are accountable, and there are several possible answers.

Accountability to children and their parents/carers

Most importantly, you are answerable to the children for the quality of your planning, teaching, assessment and feedback, for the care and guidance that you provide to them, and for ensuring that they experience equality of opportunity and the chance to fulfil their educational potential. That has always been the case for teachers.

Since primary pupils are minors, your 'clients' are the children's parents or carers. Your responsibility to them is marked formally by a legal requirement to provide written reports at least annually, and to attend parents' evenings to discuss children's work and progress. In addition to this, informal contact with parents has many potential benefits, especially in ensuring that children experience consistency of expectation and treatment between home and school. Co-operating effectively with parents is discussed in Chapter 8, where it is suggested that teachers see their relationship with parents as more than an exercise in accountability, and recognise that parents and teachers are partners in the task of raising the young.

Accountability to employers

When you are appointed to a school, you are accountable to the governing body for the way in which you perform your professional duties. A mentor and/or the head teacher will support you, and monitor and review your work against the relevant standards and against annual targets which have been agreed at the time of your annual performance review. You should be active in undertaking continuing professional development activities, in line with the expectation in Standard 8 that you will 'take responsibility for improving teaching through appropriate professional development, responding to advice and feedback from colleagues'. In the past, teachers progressed up a pay scale by virtue of automatic annual increments. In the future, decisions about your entitlement to an increment will depend on the annual appraisal of your performance. Judgements made each year by senior colleagues will check that you continue to meet the Teachers' Standards as well as your agreed targets. Failure to do so will result in a programme of support and development, but continued underperformance can lead to disciplinary action including, ultimately, dismissal.

Many teachers find their annual performance review to be a positive event, helping them to understand more accurately their strengths and weaknesses. This is particularly so when teachers take the initiative in assessing and evaluating their own performance against the Standards and their targets. If you can do this accurately, you will find your performance review to be an affirming experience, giving you increased confidence in your capability and achievement.

Accountability to your colleagues

Apart from your responsibility to your employer as an individual member of staff, your professional accountability extends to your colleagues. Within the school you are accountable to your fellow-professionals, for example by participating actively in teamwork for planning, assessing and recording. If you hold a particular responsibility, for instance as a subject leader, you share accountability with the rest of the staff for children's progress in that area of the curriculum throughout the school.

Given the increasing place of inter-professional working in the public sector, the concept of horizontal accountability (Levitt et al., 2008, p 16) has become significant. Teachers' roles in, for example, safeguarding and child protection intersect with those of colleagues in the social services, the health service and the police. Those working in these fields have a mutual accountability to one another and their work is overseen by a number of different regulatory bodies. This adds to the complexity of the notion of teachers' accountability.

Accountability to the general public

Ultimately, professionals in education are answerable to the public at large for the quality of their work. Tax payers understandably have an interest in how their money is spent. Employers expect prospective employees to be equipped with an appropriate range of core knowledge and skills, both 'hard' (such as language and number) and 'soft' (such as interpersonal skills). National and local politicians, who claim a mandate for the policies that they enact, expect positive outcomes to follow from their decisions. Your personal contribution to children's learning is reflected in inspection reports and in results published in performance tables.

Accountability to yourself

If you accept the conclusion of Levitt et al. (2008) that accountability is an ethical concept, it follows that you will need to give account to your own conscience with regard to the quality of your work. If you believe that teaching is a vocation as well as a profession, you may find that it takes over you, to the detriment of your home life and leisure activities. Finding and maintaining an appropriate work/life balance is vital. Teachers should be rounded people with a range of interests and life experience, who bring something into the school from the outside world and model to children the opportunities that lie ahead for them. While satisfying your conscience that you have done sufficient work to do a good job, make sure that you also have a fulfilling life outside school.

Limiting the scope and weight of accountability

Behn (2001) draws attention to the dangers inherent in an over-accountable profession, claiming that not even the most public-spirited government workers can succeed in an environment of rules, regulations and procedures that make it virtually impossible to perform well. Fitz (2003) agrees, contending that systems of accountability such as league tables, targets and bespoke inspection frameworks reduce teachers to 'reconstituted knowledge workers' tasked with delivering nationally determined curricula by means of imposed teaching methods. Similar responses have been made by associations representing teachers in England, for example the Association of Teachers and Lecturers (ATL) (2007).

The government, in its White Paper of 2010 (DfE, 2010), claims to have heeded warnings about over-accountability. While agreeing that schools should indeed be accountable for ensuring that pupils are educated and equipped to take their place in society, the White Paper argues that schools have suffered from a compliance regime which drove them to meet a bewildering array of centrally imposed government targets (DfE, 2010, p 66). In future, according to the White Paper, bureaucratic accountability is to be dismantled, and schools are to become more free to harness teachers' skills, judgement and enterprise. The focus of accountability will be towards parents, pupils and local communities.

It remains to be seen to what extent this commitment will be realised, given the continuing policies of published results and inspection reports which seem to pay little attention to the contextual circumstances of individual schools.

Knowing how children learn

By portraying teaching as essentially a reflective activity, this book views teachers as researchers, who are constantly reviewing their pupils' performance and their own practice in order to be able to extend children's learning and develop their own professional competence. To implement this vision in your classroom you need some grasp of key theories of learning, especially those which spring from philosophy and psychology. You also need to appreciate how to apply this theoretical knowledge to the practical task of teaching.

There is a close relationship between learning theory and subject knowledge. Chapter 3 includes a study of the types of knowledge needed by teachers, and that analysis can inform your understanding of the complex nature of learning. For example, in some lessons you may concentrate on helping children to acquire and remember key pieces of information, while in others the emphasis is on gaining and practising certain skills. Sometimes you focus on the development of attitudes, and at other times on ensuring that a fundamental concept has been fully grasped. It is because the nature of knowledge is complex that you need a sophisticated approach when using theories of learning to enhance your teaching.

The meanings of 'learning' and 'knowledge'

A typical psychological definition of learning identifies it as, 'relatively permanent changes in behaviour or in potential for behaviour that result from experience' (Lefrançois, 1999, p 41). The word 'behaviour' is being used here in a broad sense, to include both observable phenomena and changes in inner thought patterns. Some examples of changed behaviour are readily observable; for example, you can easily test a child's knowledge of multiplication facts or the meanings of words. Others are less easily measured; for instance, sophisticated questioning and observation are needed to understand a child's inner thought patterns when applying mathematical knowledge to complex problems. Lefrançois' definition consequently carries with it an implication that learning occurs at different levels. For example, a person may gain superficial knowledge of a topic by collecting pieces of factual information, or go further, in order to understand the significance of the information and the relationships among the different facts.

Bloom's (Bloom, 1956) analysis of learning proposed a six-level taxonomy, beginning with a basic demonstration of knowledge and rising through comprehension, application, analysis and synthesis to the most complex level, evaluation. Others have broadened the scope, to include intrapersonal and interpersonal factors as elements of learning (eg Gagné and Driscoll, 1988). Learning is therefore multi-layered and difficult to pin down in a single definition.

REFLECTIVE TASK

Reflecting on your teaching

»   *Select an aspect of one area of the curriculum that you have recently taught. Reflect on the extent to which you can use Bloom's six-level taxonomy of learning to identify progression in that subject, from the learning of straightforward facts and skills to the comprehension and application of the knowledge, and perhaps also to providing opportunities to bring together different pieces of learning (synthesis).*

»   *Next, look at your planning of the topic over a medium-term period. What opportunities did you include for children to acquire information, learn and practice skills, and demonstrate understanding and an ability to apply their learning to other situations?*

»   *Finally, consider whether your plans for assessment enable you to identify pupils who are working at deeper levels of learning than others.*

Knowledge is as difficult to define as learning. An analysis, in Chapter 3, of Ryle's (1949) work draws attention to factual information, skills, concepts and attitudes as different facets of knowledge, and it is clear that each of these relates to different aspects of the meaning of 'learning'. For instance, factual information can be gained at a superficial level, but conceptual understanding implies a deeper type of learning.

Markie's (2004) article summarises succinctly the key features of rationalism and empiricism, two main branches of epistemology, the branch of philosophy that studies knowledge.

*   Rationalists view knowledge as produced by rational reflection on received wisdom.

*   Empiricists see it as the product of sensory perception, and therefore related to first-hand experiences.

These different ways of regarding knowledge are reflected in the continuing debate about educational aims. Is education primarily about cultural transmission and accumulating knowledge, or is it about developing skills to facilitate the discovery or creation of knowledge? Since the inception of the English national curriculum in 1988 (DES, 1988) documentation for compulsory subjects has included both strands from this debate. The statutory curriculum is expressed in terms of what pupils should know and also what they should be able to do, reflecting both the 'body of knowledge' view and the skills-based approach.

You will notice how the philosophical debate between rationalists and empiricists has a significant influence on the question, 'what is learning?' Empiricists focus relentlessly on the importance of demonstrable truths in their understanding of knowledge. That emphasis is reflected in the concepts of fair tests in science and proofs in mathematics, and results in a definition of learning that associates it with a sceptical disposition. Empiricists insist that learning is intimately linked with proving each proposition, so that learners need to show, not simply that they know something, but also how they know it.

Rationalists counter with the argument that, although an empirical approach is a fundamental constituent of subjects such as science and mathematics, and a useful discipline in verifying factual information in other subjects, it is not universally applicable to all types of knowledge and learning. The debate between science and religion is an obvious example, but there are many others. For artists, dancers, musicians, gymnasts and poets, and for educators in literature and morality, statements which are based on judgements, opinions and beliefs for which a reasoned argument can be made are valid within their subject disciplines, even if they cannot be 'proved' to the satisfaction of an empiricist. A useful way of approaching this line of argument is to think about assessment. Examiners regularly assess the artistic merits of gymnastic routines, dance and music performances and works of art. If you were to confine assessment to what is empirically testable, then only observable behaviours would count, and judges would base their marks solely on technical detail, rather than overall performance.

Discussions between rationalists and empiricists will probably remain inconclusive, but the decision of legislators to draw on both strands of thinking when designing the curriculum is more than a pragmatic compromise. Firstly, their approach recognises the notion that each subject has its own characteristic matters and processes, accepted as valid by the community of those involved in the subject as experts. So, while the scientific community decides through continuing debate what counts as knowledge and learning in science, parallel processes taking place in other disciplines are likely to come to different conclusions. Artistic or literary merit are seen as making perfect sense in arts subjects, whereas scientists would find the concepts difficult, if not impossible, to incorporate within a theory of learning.

Secondly, as the discussion in Chapter 3 of the 'Three Wise Men' report (Alexander et al., 1992) makes clear, the practical task of covering a broad and balanced curriculum necessitates accepting an approach of cultural transmission alongside encouraging pupils to investigate and learn for themselves. Indeed Alexander et al. consider it a central part of a teacher's role to mediate the encounter between pupils' personal enquiry and the public knowledge embedded in our cultural traditions (Alexander et al., 1992, para. 64).

Learning and creativity

The notion of creativity can easily polarise opinion among those who teach.

REFLECTIVE TASK

Reflecting on alternative viewpoints

Consider the views expressed by the following two teachers.

» *Do you find yourself more in agreement with one than the other?*

» *Do you think that creativity can be taught, or does it depend upon some pre-existing potential not possessed by all?*

Retired teacher P: *Earlier in my career children seemed to have far more time to be creative than in recent years. I thought it did wonders for their confidence and their ability to express themselves. The testing regime's overemphasis on recalling information has in my view made children more compliant and less inquisitive, and that has reduced their motivation to learn and their teachers' enthusiasm for teaching.*

Retired teacher Q: *I look at it differently. I've seen far too many children whose creative skills were undermined by a lack of knowledge. For example, it's very frustrating for a child who has imaginative ideas for a story but lacks the fundamental knowledge and skills in spelling and grammar to write it. Teachers do their pupils no favours if they pretend there's a short cut to learning. Sometimes it is a chore, so we need to point out to children why it's important to gain a good command of the basics.*

There may well be a false dichotomy here. The exchange between the two retired teachers rests on an assumption that creativity and mastery of basic knowledge and skills stand in opposition to one another. The example of the composer Beethoven indicates rather that they are complementary. As a young child Beethoven displayed considerable talent in inventing new melodies on a keyboard. Instead of being given great freedom to pursue his creative talent, he was sent to study music theory intensively. He learned the current conventions about musical notation and composition, and practised writing pieces in the styles of those regarded as the pre-eminent composers of his day. Mastery of the received tradition of musical knowledge and technique provided him with the essential tools required to create his own works. His creativity rested in his ability to develop his own style, instead of simply replicating the methods of others, and the novelty of his music lies in the ways in which he systematically broke the prevailing rules of composition, the point being that he had to gain a thorough knowledge of the rules in order to be able to break them.

Retired teacher Q, quoted above, would therefore appear to be right that basic knowledge and skills are essential prerequisites for creativity, while teacher P makes an important suggestion that learners need a balance between receiving knowledge on the one hand and processing it on the other. Craft's (2010) book extends these ideas, with particular reference to the ways in which digital technology has the potential to transform both the concept of creativity and also the associated pedagogy.

If you accept the idea, outlined above, that the essential character of each subject in the curriculum is determined by its community of experts, it follows that learning the subject means being inducted into the discipline as practised by its experts. For example, in literature children should enjoy and study the poetry and prose of a range of authors, and they should also have opportunities to write for themselves in a variety of styles. In science, too, there should be a balance between learning about earlier scientific discoveries and undertaking first-hand experimental work. Interpreting learning in this way implies a need for a synthesis of didactic and heuristic approaches to teaching.

REFLECTIVE TASK

Reflecting on your reading

Whitehead, A.N. (1950) The Rhythmic Claims of Freedom and Discipline, in *The Aims of Education and Other Essays*. Second edition. London: Ernest Benn.

Read Whitehead's classic essay, in which he explores the relationship between teaching material to learners and enabling learners to assimilate it. Although Whitehead's style is difficult to penetrate (the essay was originally delivered as a public lecture in 1917), the ideas that he presents make a telling contribution to any debate about the nature of learning. Identify in his essay half a dozen quotations which express views with which you either agree or disagree. Reflecting on your responses to Whitehead's thinking, try to identify what, for you, are the essential elements of learning, on which you would wish to develop your professional practice as a primary school teacher.

The processes of learning

Psychological accounts of how learning occurs fall into two main classes, behaviourism and constructivism. Child's (2007) book, a standard text which is periodically updated, provides a full account of these, with particular reference to the application of learning theory to classroom practice. The following summaries introduce behaviourist and constructivist approaches and offer suggestions for identifying and evaluating their relevance for your own work.

Behaviourism

Because psychologists define learning in terms of what they can examine, namely changes in behaviour, they have typically examined actual behaviours in order to understand how learning occurs. An early example of this is that of Pavlov's experiment with dogs, dating from the 1890s. Pavlov sounded a bell when he fed the dogs, and noticed that by doing this repeatedly he conditioned the dogs to associate the sound of the bell with the idea that their next meal was imminent. Eventually, the sound of the bell was enough to make the dogs salivate.

Skinner (see Benjamin, 2007) demonstrated that rats could learn to operate a lever to trigger the release of a food reward. The repetition of a pattern of stimulus (the lever), response (the rats pressing it) and reward (the food) led to a change in behaviour, since the rats pressed the lever more frequently in the expectation of receiving more rewards.

These examples from Pavlov and Skinner illustrate the concept of conditioning, a fundamental term in behavioural psychology. Both experiments involve frequent repetition by the learner in the process of learning and the receipt of a reward in reinforcing what has been learned. You can readily see how this approach has influenced so-called traditional teaching, where the teacher selects and controls the material to be learned and also determines the pace of learning. An obvious example of this is rote learning, which can take the form of memorising sets of information or the repeated practice of tasks and skills.

REFLECTIVE TASKS

Reflecting on your schooldays

»   *To what extent was your primary schooling associated with memorising information so that you could readily recall it?*

»   *Were there areas of the curriculum in which regular repetition of tasks or drills was required? Identify what you see, from your own experience as a learner, as the benefits and drawbacks of that approach.*

»   *Are there any aspects of the curriculum that you now teach in which you wish that you possessed a greater store of memorised knowledge?*

Reflecting on your reading

Tait, P (2013) Rote learning is fine – there's just too much stuff to teach. *The Daily Telegraph*, 10 June, 2013.

Read Tait's (2013) article, in which he summarises what he sees as the benefits of the rote learning of information, but points to 'an explosion of information and knowledge' which makes it imperative to be more selective in what children are required to learn.

»   *How important do you think it is that members of a society have a shared set of knowledge, for example about the history and culture of the country in which they live, as a prerequisite for social discourse and cohesion? How might such a canon of knowledge be agreed upon?*

Rote learning is sometimes criticised for placing pupils in a passive role, or giving them fragments of knowledge without the means to understand it. Yet the frequent repetition of drills, such as playing scales on musical instruments or practising sequenced skills in sports, is seen as essential so that pupils can master and subsequently replicate the exercises fluently in the context of playing a musical composition or competing in a sporting activity. The same argument applies to the memorisation of number facts such as multiplication tables and addition bonds, the spelling of an extensive vocabulary, and the accumulation of a core of skills and information in each area of the curriculum, which can readily be recalled or performed. Despite attracting derogatory comment, such as 'learning parrot-fashion', rote learning is arguably an economical and efficient way of imparting information and skills, the first level of Bloom's taxonomy of learning.

The influence of behaviourism on teachers' approach to behaviour management, developed in Chapter 7, springs from the sequence of stimulus, response and reward observed in Pavlov's and Skinner's experiments. Teachers call for order, then reward compliance or punish non-compliance.

Behaviourism, motivation and relevance

When teachers employ behaviourist theory in their teaching they frequently make use of extrinsic motivation (Child, 2007, Section 3, Chapter 8), since the rewards resulting from successful learning are often unrelated to the subject matter of the lesson. For example, teachers may use praise, team points or a privilege of some sort in response to correct answers or good conduct. While primary school children usually enjoy receiving such rewards, there are dangers inherent to this approach. For example, children may perceive the goal of learning to be reward rather than achievement. By Key Stage 3 many pupils will see it as 'uncool' to receive rewards and praise from teachers, to the extent that they actively avoid such situations, and compromise their own learning. It is therefore important to incorporate intrinsic motivation into your classroom routines so that the children gain satisfaction from making progress. This is more likely to happen if you can show them that the lesson is not simply a task to be completed, but a vital step in their learning.

A closely related issue is that of relevance. Children are more likely to undertake rote tasks enthusiastically if they appreciate why they are being asked to do them. To say that an exercise must be done because it is in the textbook or the school's curriculum plans is not sufficient justification. As the teacher, you should be able to explain both the type of task, for example a practice task or an enrichment task, and what contribution it makes to a rounded education. On their own, many rote tasks appear pointless, but you can portray their value by showing their relevance to realistic situations. If pupils can link their learning to relevant contexts, they can demonstrate some of Bloom's higher-order learning attributes, such as application and comprehension. Links of this sort are essential, because unless material learned by rote is deployed and applied in other contexts it is unlikely to be retained for more than a short period of time.

Constructivism

Constructivist psychology focuses on the learner's cognitive development, and describes learning in terms of pupils' thinking, reasoning and understanding. On the basis of their findings, constructivists suggest ways in which teachers can support and enhance the process of learning.

Constructivists and stage theories

Piaget (Child, 2007, Section 2, Chapter 4) explored the perceptions of children aged three to 12. In his stage theory of learning, he suggests that children's thinking typically passes through a sequence of qualitatively different steps, and concludes that teachers should take account of the leading characteristics of the learners at each stage of their development. Central to his work is the belief that children's cognitive development occurs as they develop or construct mental models of the world, initially through their movements and sensations, next through using words and images to represent objects, then through learning to think logically about concrete events, and finally by becoming able to think abstractly and theoretically.

A feature of Piaget's thinking that has arguably been underutilised is his distinction between assimilation and accommodation. These reflect two different ways in which learners interact with their environments.

• Assimilation refers to situations in which new knowledge is incorporated into existing mental structures, thereby enlarging the learner's perspective.

• Accommodation relates to occasions when existing mental structures are changed by new, conflicting stimuli, thereby altering the learner's perspective.

You may find it helpful to bear this distinction in mind so that you provide your class with a balance between work which you consciously relate to children's previous learning and material which is entirely novel.

Criticisms of Piaget's work include drawing attention to the small, unrepresentative sample of children whom he studied, rejection of his view that development occurs inevitably and findings that many children are more able than Piaget believed they could logically be. For example, Donaldson (1978, p 30) consistently found that pre-school children were far more able to de-centre, and see another person's point of view, than Piaget thought. Many of Piaget's experiments drew upon scientific and mathematical areas of thinking, and assumed that learning takes place in small, gradual steps, whereas in some instances a sudden breakthrough in learning can lead a child to re-conceptualise a host of previous pieces of learning with the result that a substantial leap forward takes place.

A practical drawback of Piaget's thinking is that teachers may limit their expectations of learners by seeing them as 'not yet ready' to move on. This issue, discussed in Chapter 1, has a crucial bearing on the role that teachers' expectations play in determining the extent of their pupils' progress.

Kohlberg (see McLeod, 2011) built upon Piaget's work on the development of moral reasoning in children. He proposed a stage theory, discussed further in Chapter 7, which can helpfully inform your approach to behaviour management.

Constructivists and 'teaching for learning'

Bruner (1960) is usually associated with the notion of 'discovery learning'. Like Piaget, he saw children as active processors of ideas and information, who construct their own understandings, and he supported the proposition (Powell and Kalina, 2009) that teachers should not provide pupils with material in its final form, but should leave scope for them to process it for themselves, making connections with previous knowledge and making sense of new work. Some teachers have mistakenly thought that Bruner considered that the essence of education lies in allowing children the freedom to make uninhibited discoveries, but this is wide of the mark. In fact, Bruner emphasised that teachers need to select material and methods of learning and teaching in order to foster children's learning within clearly defined areas. Doing this effectively requires teachers to have an accurate picture of what pupils already know and can do, and to be able to differentiate tasks and materials to make it possible for children to perceive their connection to their prior knowledge.

Developing Piaget's stage theory approach, Bruner suggested that re-visiting topics regularly, with an emphasis on moving towards abstract levels of thinking, was a vital feature of effective learning. This notion, which gave rise to the idea of the spiral curriculum (see Chapter 4) is also related to Bruner's insistence on the importance of understanding key concepts as a key to grasping a subject (see Chapter 3). An important insight here is that a focus on helping children to develop conceptual understanding facilitates sequenced learning, rather than the accumulation of disconnected facts (Gordon, 2008).

REFLECTIVE TASK

Reflecting on alternative viewpoints

Reflect on the following conversation between a trainee teacher and the mentor.

Trainee teacher J: *My degree subject was a science, so I'm sympathetic to the idea that children should make discoveries for themselves, for instance by undertaking experiments in science. A problem that I've encountered is that children's experiments sometimes go wrong, and they don't end up with the 'right' answer. You must have met this situation. How would you handle it?*

Mentor K: *You're right. This happens quite frequently. In an ideal world you might want to review with the children how they went about the experiment, and you would almost certainly find a flaw in the design or implementation of what they'd done. However, there's seldom time to do that. Obviously, you can't allow your pupils to continue to hold a fundamental misconception, even if they have 'discovered' it for themselves, and I would probably tell them the expected outcome, and explain to them that something must have gone wrong with their experiment.*

» *How do you plan opportunities for pupils to explore material for themselves without over-planning the lesson to the extent that there is little room left for 'discovery' because the teacher has covered the possible outcomes already?*

> » *You might wish to reflect on your experiences of science lessons when you were a school pupil. Were teachers inclined to tell you the expected outcome before you did the experiment? If so, did you feel there was little point in actually completing the experiment?*

Ausubel (1968) agreed with Bruner's emphasis on teachers' ability to select appropriate material and relevant learning outcomes, but put greater weight on direct instruction, as he believed that an unvarying insistence on processing all new knowledge led to inefficiency in teaching. He was also concerned to avoid a common criticism levelled at constructivists, that they require learners to 'reinvent the wheel' by 'discovering' knowledge that has been known for generations. An area of strong agreement between Bruner and Ausubel lies in the importance that both placed on helping learners to create links between new material and what they already know. Ausubel's judgement that

> *the most important single factor influencing learning is what the learner already knows. Ascertain this and teach him accordingly*

> (Ausubel, 1968, p vi)

enshrines his lasting legacy to education, and directly influences the second bulleted point in Standard 2, which requires teachers to 'be aware of pupils' capabilities and their prior knowledge, and plan teaching to build on these'.

Social constructivism

Vygotsky wrote in Russian in the 1920s and 1930s, and his work remained largely unknown in the West until translated in the 1970s. Central to his work is the concept of cultural mediation (Vygotsky, 1978). Whereas Piaget, Bruner and Ausubel studied the interactions between learners and the material to be learned, Vygotsky examined the process of interactions through which children are inducted into the thoughts, values and customs of their cultures. He found that contact with parents, other significant adults including teachers, and wider social groups all play a part in the process.

The Zone of Proximal Development (ZPD) is a key component of Vygotsky's thinking. It refers to the difference between what learners can know or do independently, and what they can achieve with support from a more knowledgeable person, such as a teacher. He found the degree of progress made to be proportional to the extent of the support provided, especially in the initial stages of learning something new. The support provided by the teacher, which he called 'scaffolding', could incorporate a variety of teaching activities, including clarifying intended learning outcomes, breaking tasks into more manageable components, monitoring progress and giving feedback on errors. As pupils became competent and confident in a task, the amount of support provided by the teacher could be decreased to the point where learners could work independently.

An implication of this approach is that teachers should differentiate the amount and type of scaffolding provided for different groups and individuals in a class. This may be more important than differentiating the content of the lesson. This aspect of Vygotsky's thinking should influence teachers' expectations of their pupils. Variations in educational outcomes among pupils from different socio-economic backgrounds have long been noted. Economic advantage, parental aspiration and guidance, and community influences are contributory factors. The emphasis in the Teachers' Standards on the need to have high expectations of all pupils, discussed in Chapter 1, is framed with such scenarios in mind.

Whereas teachers might conclude, based on Piaget's stage theory, that they should wait for learners to reach an appropriate stage of development before introducing new ideas, Vygotsky's emphasis on the influence of social context upon learning suggests that active intervention by teachers is fundamentally important in moving pupils forward in their learning. Powell and Kalina's (2009) article argues cogently for the integration of constructivist and social constructivist approaches as a means of ensuring that the individual learner acquires knowledge in realistic contexts and learns with and from others.

Learning, the brain and learning styles

Neuroscience has advanced rapidly in recent years with regard to understanding the brain and its working. Particularly interesting to teachers is the idea that different areas of the brain are involved simultaneously when a task is undertaken, with neurons networking with one another to 'fire' the synapses. The notion of 'connectedness', identified earlier in the chapter, is again seen as a key component in learning. However, Sharp and Murphy's (2006, p 39) comment that 'the working of the human brain is simply far too complex to formulate any sensible, practical, everyday educational application' is probably, for the present, a pragmatic conclusion. While there appears to be much potential in future collaboration between neuroscientists and educators, the field is not yet sufficiently developed to offer a secure basis on which to establish professional practice. Indeed, myths and misconceptions abound in this contested area, and it would appear that, compared with behaviourism and constructivism, the impact of neuroscience on pedagogy is in its infancy.

A notable example of attempts to apply neuroscience to classroom practice is that surrounding learning styles. Cassidy (2004) warns that pedagogical approaches based on a threefold typology of learning styles, visual, auditory and kinaesthetic (VAK), are based on misconceptions of the work of cognitive psychologists and neuroscientists. This critique provides a useful set of criteria against which to judge VAK instruments used in some schools. In any case, the following teacher, who commented on the VAK debate, would appear to have asked a significant question.

REFLECTIVE TASK

Reflecting on alternative viewpoints

Consider the points made by this teacher.

» *To what extent do you agree with her evaluation of a VAK approach to learning styles?*

Teacher G: *A colleague tried to tell me that learners usually have a bent towards a particular type of learning style, and we ought to provide them with material in the style that best suits them. We're either visual learners, or auditory learners, or kinaesthetic learners. I can appreciate where she's coming from, but so what? If someone is good at learning from what they see, should I always give them materials with plenty of illustrations? Or should I try to make them a more rounded learner by helping them to improve their listening skills? I can accept that people are not equally good at different approaches to learning, but that doesn't mean we should imprison them in one style, simply because they seem best at it.*

Involving children in their own learning

The truism that learning is something done by learners, not to them, is a statement with which constructivists in particular would agree. An important part of your role as a teacher goes beyond monitoring and assessing your pupils' learning. Involvement in understanding the processes of their own learning, and in making realistic judgements about their achievements, can provide stimulus, motivation and feedback for children. King (1991) showed how addressing pupils' metacognitive skills, by instructing children in strategic questioning, led to improvements in their problem-solving abilities, as they took control of the piece of learning for themselves.

Well-structured lessons will include opportunities for pupils to comprehend the intended learning outcomes, and to reflect on how well they have met them. Through discussion with pupils of their achievements you are able to bolster the confidence of some and check the over-confidence of others. The use of ipsative assessment (Harlen and James, 1997) can be invaluable in encouraging children to measure their own progress in relation to their prior achievement, and is a valuable means of helping them to become self-motivated learners. Schools which use it as part of their assessment policy and procedures often incorporate it in their approach to marking. For example, children may write a brief evaluation of their work at the end of the piece to be marked. The teacher, in addition to making an assessment of the work, will also respond to the pupils' comments, to moderate their judgements and suggest future areas for attention.

Performance of understanding

Thinking about the school in which you work or have recently worked, respond to the prompts after each intended learning outcome, as a means of identifying your knowledge and understanding of the issues covered in the chapter.

- *an appreciation of a teacher's accountability for children's learning;*
  - . Identify an occasion when your performance as a teacher was reviewed by a more senior professional. By what criteria was the quality of your work measured? What part did you play in evaluating your own performance?
  - Find in the school handbook any agreed policies and procedures for communicating with parents. Evaluate your own contacts with parents, looking

for evidence of subsequent benefit to their children's learning. To what extent do you regard your conversations with parents as confidential, and when, if ever, would you share them with other members of staff?

- *a knowledge of how a range of theories of learning can help you to plan, conduct and evaluate your work;*

  - What sorts of information and skills do you expect children to be able to recall or reproduce readily? Reflecting on your recent teaching, identify one or two examples in which you used rote learning with your class. What was the educational value of these occasions? How did you enable the children to see the relevance of the tasks?

  - Identify in your recent teaching examples of planning which reflect Piaget's notions of assimilation and accommodation. To what extent can these concepts help you to ensure a balance in your children's learning between material which extends their existing knowledge and ideas that challenge them to reformulate their thinking?

- *an understanding of the importance of matching your teaching plans to pupils' capabilities and prior knowledge;*

  - Looking at your recent planning for an area of the curriculum, reflect on the extent to which you were able to identify pupils' existing knowledge and capability in that topic. Although records from their earlier learning may indicate attainment of key objectives, learners may be unable to recall some of their prior achievements. What do you do to establish whether prior coverage of a topic has led to secure knowledge?

  - Arising from Vygotsky's suggestion that children's varied social interactions are crucial in their learning, identify one or two examples when you used very different levels of scaffolding to support groups and individuals in your class. Reflect on your justification for doing so.

- *an awareness of techniques for involving children in understanding, monitoring and evaluating their own work;*

  - In what ways does your approach to marking encourage children to evaluate and comment on their own work? Identify some examples of this in practice, and reflect on the extent to which, in your view, pupils have an accurate view of their achievement.

  - Identify an example in which you employed a metacognitive approach in your teaching, by teaching children how to learn, rather than what to learn. Reflect on ways in which you could build on this way of working, in order to enable pupils to gain a fuller understanding of their own learning.

Taking it further

Benjamin, L T (2007) *A Brief History of Modern Psychology*. Oxford: Blackwell.

Child, D (ed) (2007) *Psychology and the Teacher*. Eighth edition. London: Continuum.

Raiker, A (2007) Cognitive Development in Zwozdiak-Myers, P (ed) *Childhood and Youth Studies.* Exeter: Learning Matters.

References

Alexander, R, Rose, J and Woodhead, C (1992) *Curriculum Organisation and Classroom Practice in Primary Schools: A Discussion Paper.* London: DES.

Association of Teachers and Lecturers (ATL) (2007) *New Accountability for Schools; A Position Statement.* London: ATL.

Ausubel, D P (1968) *Educational Psychology: A Cognitive View.* New York: Holt, Rinehart and Winston.

Behn, R D (2001) *Rethinking Democratic Accountability.* Washington, DC: The Brookings Institute.

Benjamin, L T (2007) *A Brief History of Modern Psychology.* Oxford: Blackwell.

Bloom, B (1956) *Taxonomy of Educational Objectives: The Classification of Educational Goals, Handbook 1, Cognitive Domain.* New York: David McKay.

Bovens, M (2005) Public Accountability, in Ferlie, E, Lynn, L E and Pollitt, C (eds) *The Oxford Handbook of Public Management.* Oxford: Oxford University Press.

Bruner, J S (1960) *The Process of Education.* Cambridge, MA: Harvard University Press.

Cassidy, S (2004) Learning Styles: An Overview of Theories, Models and Measures. *Educational Psychology*, 24 (4): 419–44.

Child, D (ed) (2007) *Psychology and the Teacher.* Eighth edition. London: Continuum.

Craft, A (2010) *Creativity and Education Futures: Learning in a Digital Age.* Stoke-on-Trent: Trentham.

Department for Education (DfE) (2010) *The Importance of Teaching – The Schools White Paper 2010.* CM 7980. London: DfE.

Department of Education and Science (DES) (1988) *The Education Reform Act, 1988.* London: DES.

Donaldson, M (1978) *Children's Minds.* London: Fontana.

Fitz, J (2003) The Politics of Accountability: A Perspective from England and Wales. *Journal of Education*, 78 (4): 230–41.

Gagné, R M and Driscoll, M P (1988) *Essentials of Learning for Instruction.* Englewood Cliffs, NJ: Prentice Hall.

Gordon, M (2008) Between Constructivism and Connectedness. *Journal of Teacher Education*, 59 (4): 322–31.

Harlen, W and James, M (1997) Assessment and Learning: Differences and Relationships between Formative and Summative Assessment. *Assessment in Education: Principles, Policy and Practice*, 4 (3): 365–79.

King, A (1991) Effects of Training in Strategic Questioning on Children's Problem Solving Performance. *Journal of Educational Psychology*, 83: 307–17.

Lefrançois, G R (1999) *Psychology for Teaching.* Tenth edition. Belmont, CA: Wadsworth.

Levitt, R, Janta, B and Wegrich, K (2008) *Accountability of Teachers: Literature Review.* Cambridge: Rand Europe.

Markie, P (2004) Rationalism versus Empiricism, in Zalta, E D (ed) *Stanford Encyclopedia of Philosophy*. Available online at http://plato.stanford.edu/entries/rationalism-empiricism (accessed 13 November 2013).

McLeod, S A (2011) *Kohlberg – Moral Development – Simply Psychology*. Available online at www.simplypsychology.org/kohlberg.html (accessed 15 November 2013).

Powell, K C and Kalina, C J (2009) Cognitive and Social Constructivism: Developing Tools for An Effective Classroom. *Education*, 130 (2): 241–50.

Ryle, G (1949) *The Concept of Mind*. London: Hutchinson.

Sharp, J and Murphy, B (2006) The Mystery of Learning, in Sharp, J, Ward, S and Hankin, L (eds) *Education Studies: An Issues Based Approach*. Exeter: Learning Matters.

Tait, P (2013) Rote learning is fine – there's just too much stuff to teach. *The Daily Telegraph*, 10 June 2013.

Vygotsky, L S (1978) *Mind in Society: The Development of Higher Psychological Processes*. Cambridge, MA: Harvard University Press.

Whitehead, A N (1950) The Rhythmic Claims of Freedom and Discipline, in *The Aims of Education and Other Essays*. Second edition. London: Ernest Benn.

3 Subject and curriculum knowledge

Learning outcomes

By the end of this chapter you should have developed and clarified:

- *an appreciation of the nature of subjects and their contribution to human experience and understanding;*

- *an awareness of the relationship between subject knowledge and pedagogical subject knowledge;*

- *your knowledge of the whole curriculum, and of the place within it of the national curriculum; and*

- *an understanding of the knowledge that you need in order to teach the whole curriculum, with particular attention to English and mathematics.*

Introduction

At first sight, Standard 3, 'a teacher must demonstrate good subject and curriculum knowledge', appears obvious and straightforward. It is self-evident that primary school teachers need accurate knowledge of the material that pupils are supposed to learn during Key Stages 1 and 2. Given the spread of subjects taught in primary schools, that is no mean feat. However, you might also readily agree that teachers should know what children will have been taught during the Early Years Foundation Stage (EYFS), so that they can build upon it, and at least possess an outline of the secondary school curriculum at Key Stage 3, if not beyond.

Moving from stage to stage in education contains a risk that discontinuity may result in a loss of momentum in children's learning. For this reason, transitions between phases of education have been extensively studied in recent years. Sanders et al. (2005) identify key issues facing schools when dealing with the move from the EYFS to Key Stage 1. Allingham (2011) offers a valuable mapping exercise demonstrating the transition from the seven areas of learning and development prescribed for the EYFS (DfE, 2012) to the Key Stage 1 curriculum. Galton et al. (2003) emphasise the importance of careful planning and cooperation between primary and secondary teachers at times of transition, because they found a significant dip in educational performance during the first year of secondary education, and Sutherland et al. (2010) provide a detailed study of primary/secondary transition, offering various models of good practice. Whereas it might be tempting to concentrate on children's social and emotional needs when they transfer between schools, these authors all highlight the significance of curriculum continuity. At a time when everything else is changing – school, teachers, classmates, rules and routines – a familiar curriculum in terms of both content and teaching methods can make the transition smooth and maintain pupils' progress.

Knowing the primary curriculum and the transitions at either end of it would be a good start, but there is much more to consider. What level of subject knowledge do you need as a teacher? What makes subjects different from one another? Are the traditional subjects a sufficient basis for a modern primary education? How do subjects interrelate? Is a 'curriculum area' different from a subject, and if so, how? What is meant by 'curriculum'? In England, the diversification of the school system marked by the establishment of academies and free schools means that increasing numbers of schools have the freedom to define their own curricula, and this offers both opportunity and challenge to teachers.

Knowing the curriculum

'Curriculum' has been an over-worked word in educational debate since the 1980s, often to the exclusion of a consideration of educational aims. The curriculum that you and your colleagues provide is designed to move the pupils towards the achievement of some long-term aims, for example to encourage them to become life-long learners, to prepare them for the opportunities and responsibilities of adult life, to equip them for the world of work or to enable them to fulfil worthwhile potentials. Aims such as this, often encapsulated in a school's mission statement or vision statement, ought to be kept in mind when you think about the curriculum, which is the main vehicle provided by the school in order to address its vision.

Consider three aspects of the curriculum.

1. The *formal* curriculum is the planned programmes of work in the various subjects taught at the school, together with other compulsory features of school life such as collective worship, the school's rules and routines, and educational visits provided as part of the taught programmes.

2. The *informal* curriculum consists of activities which are planned but not compulsory, for example after-school clubs and societies, and optional excursions offered as 'extras' outside of school hours: in short, those things that are often described as *'extra-curricular'*.

3. The *hidden* curriculum refers to unplanned, unintended consequences that impact on children's learning. Examples include the positive and negative effects of teachers' personalities upon their relationships with their classes, or the inferences

drawn by pupils from a teacher's decision to display some children's work on the wall and to exclude the work of others.

This chapter deals principally with the formal curriculum. The informal and hidden curricula are dealt with in Chapter 5, but your grasp of the wider curriculum is an important factor in your knowledge. The national curriculum in England, introduced in 1988 and subsequently reviewed several times, has never been envisaged as the whole curriculum. If your classes are to benefit from the broad, balanced curriculum envisaged in education legislation, you will need to develop and keep under review a vision of the total educational experience that you believe children need.

Knowing the subjects: the traditional curriculum

Subject knowledge defies simple definition. Subjects are inherently complex; they also differ from one another in their logical structures and their purposes in human societies. In England, particularly close attention has been paid since the 1980s to the subjects making up the primary school curriculum, following a national debate initiated by Prime Minister James Callaghan in 1976 (*The Guardian*, 2001). Central to the debate was a concern that the curriculum should keep pace with the rapid changes taking place in employment opportunities. This has influenced the evolution of the curriculum, not so much with respect to the names of the subjects studied in school (which, apart from the various areas of technology, have changed little in a century), but in terms of the particular areas within subjects selected for school syllabuses.

REFLECTIVE TASKS

Reflecting on your reading

The Guardian (2001) Towards a National Debate: Full Text of a Speech by Prime Minister James Callaghan at Ruskin College, Oxford, on 18 October, 1976. *The Guardian,* 15 October 2001.

Read Callaghan's speech (reproduced in *The Guardian* on the 25th anniversary of the occasion).

» *Identify the grounds that he gave for raising concerns about current school curricula and teaching methods in 1976.*

» *Do you consider that any similar concerns are evident today?*

Notice that Callaghan has plenty to say about the aims of a nation's education system, although these became hidden in the welter of discussion that ensued, which focused on what should be included in the formal curriculum.

» *To what extent do you agree with what Callaghan says about educational aims and goals? Do they need revision in the light of today's circumstances?*

Reflecting on alternative viewpoints

Consider the views of these people, including two whose teaching careers spanned the past 30 or 40 years:

Retired head teacher P: *In the aftermath of Callaghan's speech I and many of my colleagues saw it as an attack on our professionalism, and a precursor to the imposition upon us of a curriculum designed by politicians and civil servants. For the rest of my career I rather resented the restriction on my ability to use my judgement and initiative.*

Head teacher Q: *I didn't start teaching until 1990, so I've known nothing but a nationally prescribed curriculum. Reading Callaghan's speech dispassionately, I can see that there was some justification in calling the school curriculum a 'secret garden', because there was then no obvious means of collecting the input of stakeholders, especially employers and industrialists, when deciding what should be taught in school. I'm not sure that much has changed in that respect.*

Retired head teacher R: *I tend to agree with you. Before the national curriculum, much of the impetus for the academic subjects came from what children would need to do to get up to A level standard – and that at a time when a much smaller percentage of youngsters took A levels. The education system was akin to a parallel universe in comparison with the world of work.*

» *How do you think the school curriculum should be shaped, and by whom?*

» *What does that tell you about the aims of education that you profess?*

» *And what does it tell you about what you need to know as a primary teacher?*

The national debate instigated by Callaghan gave rise to a great deal of work, spearheaded by Her Majesty's Inspectorate (HMI) (1985), designed to identify an appropriate curriculum for pupils in England from five to 16, and led ultimately to the national curriculum, introduced in 1988 (DES, 1988). The HMI publication, a major contribution to the debate, set out key principles for describing and discussing the curriculum, and it was accompanied by a separate volume for each subject. Much of the groundwork for this series of booklets centred on analysing subjects in terms of knowledge, skills, concepts and attitudes, drawing upon the work of Ryle (1949).

Ryle's analysis of the nature of knowledge emphasises that it is inadequate to think of any subject as simply a collection of pieces of information, the learning of which will lead to mastery of the subject. While it is true that factual information is at the heart of all subjects, it is also the case that learning each subject entails the acquisition and practice of a set of skills, and that each discipline can nurture a set of subject-specific attitudes. Additionally, and fundamental to Ryle's thinking, every subject displays a set of key concepts, or central ideas, around which the subject is organised, which make sense of its factual components and its associated attitudes and skills, and which ensure its coherence.

One example can serve to illustrate and simplify the complex impression made by Ryle's analysis. In mathematics, the pieces of information include the facts that 2 + 3 = 5 and 6 + 4 = 10. A mathematical skill, learned initially with a box of bricks, an abacus or the fingers of two hands, and later internalised so that no apparatus is required, is the ability to combine two numbers to make one, larger number. Another, more general, skill is the ability to apply these facts and processes to everyday situations and problems. Doing this can and should nurture an attitude of concern for detail and accuracy. The fundamental concept behind this aspect of mathematics is of course that of addition. This concept, alongside others such as subtraction, multiplication, division, ratio and percentages, re-appears regularly in the mathematics syllabus, at increasing levels of complexity. Thus, learners may start by combining two single-digit numbers, then proceed to learn pairs of numbers that add up to ten, and next explore algorithms enabling them to add numbers up to hundreds, then thousands. Later still come addition exercises involving fractions, negative numbers and algebraic symbols; applications relating to the measurement of length, area, volume, capacity, angles and time; and calculations involving money.

Notice how the concept of addition acts as an organising principle which unlocks for learners a host of facts and figures and procedures as they work their way through the mathematics syllabus. Comparable examples may be indentified in other concepts in mathematics, and in the concepts embedded in all the other subjects.

The central role of concepts in understanding subjects

In a classic text, Bruner (1960) explores the major issues relevant to teachers' subject knowledge, and identifies conceptual understanding as crucial. He regards a subject's key concepts as the pillars holding up its framework of knowledge and skills, examples being cause and effect in history, rhythm and pitch in music, and faith and worship in religion. He gives four main reasons for regarding such concepts, or 'fundamentals' as he terms them, as particularly significant.

1. Firstly, their role as organising principles helps to make the subject comprehensible. In other words, you can see different pieces of information as examples of a single concept.

2. Secondly, they enable you to arrange detailed material in a structured way, which helps you to remember it.

3. Thirdly, they promote transfer of training, because you can see new material as a fresh example of a concept that you encountered previously, and this helps you to access it and understand it.

4. Finally, arranging a subject on a skeleton of concepts helps to narrow the gap between elementary and advanced knowledge, so that you can learn it more quickly.

The challenge of using a subject's key concepts as a basis for extending and consolidating your own knowledge is a valuable discipline, because it helps you to organise in a systematic way the sheer quantity of material that you need to know in order to teach the primary curriculum. It also helps enormously in the task of planning well-structured lessons and series of lessons (see Chapter 4).

REFLECTIVE TASK

Reflecting on your teaching

»   Review your recent medium-term planning for one subject of your choice, and identify one of the subject's key concepts that you addressed in the sequence of lessons.

»   Reflect on the ways in which your pupils may have encountered this concept at an earlier stage in their learning of the subject, including during the EYFS. Could you have improved your approach to planning by building more consciously upon those prior experiences?

»   Consider what future opportunities the children will have to enlarge their understanding of the concept later in their schooling, including during Key Stage 3.

»   Scrutinise the documentation, nationally provided or school generated, used in your school for planning the curriculum in the subject. To what extent does it make explicit reference to key concepts?

Acquainting yourself with the key concepts embedded in each of the subjects that you teach ought to provide you with a framework on which to hang everything else you need to know about the subject – its facts, skills and attitudes, and the distinctive language and vocabulary specific to the discipline. Concept maps (Birbili, 2006) for each of the subjects can display the relationships among the different areas of the subject, and help you to identify relevant links between one subject and another. They can also be a useful teaching device, illuminating children's understanding of a subject, and identifying major misconceptions that they may hold (see Chapter 6).

Pedagogical subject knowledge

Knowing a subject is one thing. Knowing it in a way that enables you to teach it effectively is another. Central to the notion of pedagogical subject knowledge, or pedagogical content knowledge, as it is sometimes called (Shulman, 1986), is the necessity of integrating the 'what' and the 'how' of teaching. Nothing is more frustrating for learners than to be taught by a teacher with superb subject knowledge, but who lacks the ability to convey the subject to the class, often owing to a failure to select appropriately from the mass of their knowledge, or to a lack of awareness of the developmental stages of the learners.

A teacher's ability to provide pupils with continuity in the curriculum that they encounter, and progression in the learning activities designed for them, is vital. In some subjects, for example mathematics and science, the order in which material is introduced to learners is crucial, since encountering certain sequential steps is an integral feature of the subject. In others, the order in which topics occur is less important, but the task of pitching material at an appropriate level remains significant. As well as knowing subjects yourself, you also need to know ways in which learners can most fruitfully encounter them at different levels – a very tall order indeed.

If you are to assess learning, in the light of Lefrançois' definition of learning as 'relatively permanent changes in behaviour' (Lefrançois, 1999, p 41), you need to be able to measure both observable and unseen changes in behaviour. For example, you can easily assess an ability to spell words, define mathematical terms or describe scientific experiments by means of a paper and pencil test or an oral question and answer session. However, it is much harder to investigate pupils' comprehension of passages of literature, their processes of reasoning in solving mathematical problems or their insight into interpretations of data in scientific experiments, since these involve changes in unseen thought patterns.

These examples portray different levels of learning, and are reflected in Bloom's (1956) taxonomy of educational objectives, considered in Chapter 2. The complexity inherent in the meaning of 'learning' is mirrored by related complexities inherent to each subject. Pedagogical subject knowledge is about bringing together your knowledge of the subject, your knowledge of how learners learn and an appreciation of different levels of learning, from superficial to deep learning. There is a close relationship between this imperative and Bruner's (1960) notion of the spiral curriculum, explored in Chapter 4.

The limitations of a subject-based curriculum: the connectedness of knowledge

Whitehead (1950), in an essay originally delivered as a lecture in 1916, claimed that 'education is the acquisition of the art of the utilisation of knowledge' (p 6). He protested against an education system overloaded with 'inert ideas', which he characterised as 'ideas that are merely received into the mind without being utilised, or tested, or thrown into fresh combinations' (p 1f), and called for the eradication of 'the fatal disconnection of subjects which kills the vitality of our modern curriculum' (p 10). Whitehead's ideas could well form the basis of a reflective critique of education in England, almost a century after he delivered his lecture.

The decades since Callaghan's (1976) Ruskin College speech can be characterised as an era of curriculum formulation and re-formulation founded, especially since 1988, on the re-affirmation of a compartmentalised, subject-based view of knowledge. Ironically, despite Callaghan's call for the curriculum to encompass preparation for work as one of several appropriate goals of education, employers continue to claim that school leavers lack key skills (Elliott, 2011), while attainment in literacy and numeracy among 16- to 24-year olds was judged in 2013 to be almost the lowest in the developed world (Garner, 2013). Whitehead's analysis would suggest that urgent attention should be paid to the connectedness of knowledge, both to show how subjects relate to one another and also to focus on the application of knowledge to contexts beyond the school. The duty to foster and maintain children's interest in subjects, explicitly mentioned in the bulleted exemplification of Standard 3, is greatly helped if teachers can show children realistic applications of what is being taught.

White's (2005) claim that 'there is no good reason for basing curriculum planning centrally around school subjects or forms of knowledge' (p 143) seems at first sight rather startling. Pointing out that the national curriculum of 1988 was virtually devoid of aims (p 138) he concludes that it represented an unquestioning re-affirmation of a traditional curriculum, which he traces back to the dissenting academies of the eighteenth century. The consequence is what he calls a 'Janus-faced curriculum' (p 138). On one side, the subject-based curriculum unthinkingly preserves a received tradition; on the other, the aspirations of individuals and communities are expressed as goals extrinsic to the school system, and often utilitarian in purpose. A consequence of this is that academic subjects, such as history, design technology and languages, sit uneasily alongside other areas of the curriculum such as personal, social, health and economic education. For a variety of reasons the former appear to have greater status in the curriculum hierarchy than the latter, which are consequently relegated to an unimportant status by teachers and pupils alike.

White's comments are consistent with a view that the 'secret garden' of the school curriculum, of which Callaghan complained in 1976, has survived decades of reform, and still fails to respond to the expressed needs of society. His conclusion is that the task of curriculum design, as a constantly evolving process, ought to follow on from the articulation and clarification of agreed aims. Unless the goals of education are clear, curriculum development is destined to fail.

REFLECTIVE TASKS

Reflecting on alternative viewpoints

»   *Consider the responses of two of the retired head teachers quoted earlier in the chapter when they were questioned about White's notion of a 'Janus-faced curriculum':*

Retired head teacher P: *Alongside the national curriculum subjects, there was always an expectation that schools would do more than teach formal subjects. Road safety, healthy eating, economic and industrial understanding, personal and social education, sex and relationships are just a few of the things that come to mind. Because it took us almost all of our time to teach the statutory subjects, I always felt we were squeezing these other things in, and not doing them justice.*

Retired head teacher R: *Yes, and we wasted a lot of time auditing the 'extras' to show that they contributed to the national curriculum subjects. Ironically, the so-called 'extras' tended to be the topics that made education relevant for the children, and corresponded with life outside school. But they usually took second place because of the emphasis on traditional subjects, especially when Ofsted began to inspect on a subject-by-subject basis.*

Reflecting on your teaching

Examine what you have taught over a period of, say, a month.

»   *To what extent does White's description of a 'Janus-faced' curriculum fit with your practice?*

»   *Do the recollections of the two retired head teachers resonate with your current experience, or have circumstances changed?*

Reflecting on your schooldays

Consider your perception of the curriculum that you received as a primary school pupil.

» *Which aspects were portrayed as more or less important?*

» *What do you think your teachers needed to know about the curriculum that they taught?*

» *What do you consider to be the greatest changes in the demands made upon teachers' subject knowledge between your schooldays and your present situation?*

The arguments advanced by Whitehead and White illustrate a central conundrum facing designers of curricula. The issue is where to start. Should you begin from a standpoint of cultural transmission, by defining the knowledge, skills and understandings that ought to be passed from one generation to the next? Or should you begin with an analysis of how children learn, then articulate what they need to know if they are to play a full part in society and lead fulfilling lives? In other words, do you start from subjects or from children?

Notice that both of these approaches are based upon fundamental aims, and also that the former can readily be aligned with a behaviourist view of teaching and learning, and the latter with a constructivist standpoint (see Chapter 2). Alexander, Rose and Woodhead (1992), in the influential 'Three Wise Men' report, claim that the two aims are not mutually exclusive. The value of a cultural transmission approach is that subjects represent 'some of the most powerful tools for making sense of the world which human beings have ever devised' (para 64) and these should not be denied to children. The value of beginning with how children learn is in taking seriously the task of systematically expanding pupils' horizons by enabling them to make sense of their experiences. The 'Three Wise Men' conclude that

> While it is self-evident that every individual, to an extent, constructs his/her meanings, education is an encounter between these personal understandings and the public knowledge embodied in our cultural traditions. The teacher's key responsibility is to mediate such encounters so that the child's understanding is enriched.

> (para 64)

Viewing the teacher as a mediator, who brings children and subjects together, is an important insight. It promotes a synthesis between behaviourist and constructivist approaches to teaching and learning, a re-statement of the importance of pedagogical subject knowledge and a potential means of resolving the dilemma encapsulated in White's reference to a 'Janus-faced curriculum'.

Connecting the curriculum

A recent resurgence of interest in cross-curricular planning reflects a concern to bridge the divide between a subject-centred and a child-centred curriculum. Rose (2009), in the final report of an independent review of the primary curriculum prepared for the Labour government of the time, found that excellence in the basics, which he defined as literacy, numeracy, ICT skills and personal development (Rose, 2009, Section 1.2, p 2), is crucial for enabling children to access a broad and balanced curriculum, but he further reported that

> *Our primary schools also show that high standards are best secured when essential knowledge and skills are learned both through direct, high-quality subject teaching and also through this content being applied and used in cross-curricular studies. Primary schools have long organised and taught much of the curriculum as a blend of discrete subjects and cross-curricular studies in this way. It is the best of this work that has informed the recommendations of this review.*
>
> (Rose, 2009, Section 1.2, p 2f)

Once a key strategy deployed by primary teachers prior to the national curriculum of 1988, cross-curricular topic work fell from favour partly because the statutory curriculum and Ofsted's inspection methodology reinforced subject teaching, and partly because cross-curricular planning all too often revealed shallow subject knowledge on the part of teachers, resulting in patchy coverage of subjects and spurious links across them. At its best, however, this approach has the potential to enable children to see their experiences and their studies as contributing to their knowledge of different disciplines simultaneously. But the demands that it makes upon your subject knowledge should not be underestimated.

REFLECTIVE TASKS

Reflecting on your reading

Alexander, R, Rose, J and Woodhead, C (1992) *Curriculum Organisation and Classroom Practice in Primary Schools: A Discussion Paper.* London: DES.

This important report provides a detailed critique of cross-curricular approaches (paragraphs 62 to 72 on pp 21–23). Read these sections and identify what their arguments imply about the types of subject knowledge needed by teachers if cross-curricular planning is to succeed.

Skim-read Kelly and Stead (2013), which offers examples of rigorous cross-curricular planning arising from a science syllabus, and consider Ewens (2011, pp 158–62), which outlines a number of case studies demonstrating how a focus on a local community provided a realistic context for work that included several different subjects. In each of Ewens' cases, the teachers' starting point for planning was their knowledge of the pupils' developmental stages and interests. Subject knowledge came into play at a later stage.

» *What challenges would the types of approach outlined in these texts make to your own subject knowledge?*

Reflecting on your teaching

Thinking about the lessons that you taught on one recent day, decide what answers you would give to children who asked, 'why did we need to learn that?' Your knowledge of the curriculum ought to be such that you can perceive links to situations extrinsic to the school.

The primary national curriculum from September 2014

Following the change of government in 2010, the incoming Secretary of State for Education instituted a further review of the national curriculum. This process has resulted in a revised curriculum for primary schools in England. It is compulsory in maintained schools, but other schools such as academies and free schools are at liberty to design their own curricula. Although at first sight the new arrangements (DfE, 2013) might give the impression of a return to a traditional subject-based curriculum, a close reading of the framework document for the primary curriculum tells a rather different story.

1. Firstly, the policy context of the curriculum's statutory guidance is described as 'reforming qualifications and the curriculum to better prepare pupils for life after school' (DfE, 2013, p 1). By linking the curriculum to the extrinsic interests of society this statement clearly implies an intention to bridge the gap identified in White's description of a 'Janus curriculum', and so avoid a disconnection between traditional subjects and areas of knowledge and skill relevant to daily living.

2. Secondly, the relationship between the whole curriculum and the national curriculum is defined and emphasised, making it clear that the subject-based curriculum is part of a greater entity: 'The school curriculum comprises all learning and other experiences that each school plans for its pupils. The national curriculum forms one part of the school curriculum' (DfE, 2013, Section 2.2, p 5).

3. Thirdly, detailed subject-by-subject prescription has been greatly reduced in the foundation subjects. In English and mathematics there is still substantial direction, and in science a detailed programme of study, but other foundation subjects have outline programmes of study which are much briefer than in previous versions of the national curriculum. The rationale for this approach is that 'the national curriculum provides an outline of core knowledge around which teachers can develop exciting and stimulating lessons to promote the development of pupils' knowledge, understanding and skills as part of the wider school curriculum' (DfE, 2013, Section 3.2, p 6). This provision indicates a greater role for teachers' professional judgement when designing curricula than in previous versions of the national curriculum.

4. Fourthly, the importance of language and literacy, and of number and mathematics, across the whole curriculum is strongly emphasised. Fluency in these subjects is seen as vital in ensuring access to the rest of the curriculum, and their application to realistic situations is advocated.

If you re-read Callaghan's (1976) Ruskin College speech, then read the first 11 pages of the 2014 primary national curriculum document, you may well conclude that the latest version of the national curriculum comes close to implementing the reforms that Callaghan wanted, almost 40 years after he initiated the 'great debate'.

The reduction in the level of prescription in the 2014 curriculum is likely to present schools with some practical problems. A generation of teachers trained for a more prescriptive curriculum, characterised by Twiselton (2006) as 'curriculum deliverers' (see Chapter 4), will need to adapt to the freedom to create curricula for their pupils. You may find the work done by Rose (2009) at the request of the previous government to be of considerable value in this respect, especially in the annexes to his report which suggest cross-curricular links relevant to each subject. These sections offer guidance about making appropriate links across the curriculum. Familiarising yourself with Rose's suggestions will provide a good springboard from which to launch ideas of your own.

The 2014 national curriculum: implications for your subject knowledge

It follows from a consideration of the nature of the 2014 national curriculum that your knowledge of subjects and other curriculum areas should exhibit the following characteristics:

1. Firstly, a thorough knowledge and understanding of the detailed curriculum for English, and of the requirements for language and literacy which underpin teaching and learning throughout the curriculum. It is important not to restrict your knowledge to what is prescribed for the year group that you are currently teaching, since any class will include pupils working at levels above and below those described as typical for the age group.

2. Secondly, a parallel knowledge and understanding of the detailed curriculum for mathematics, and of the requirements for number which underpin teaching and learning throughout the curriculum. Knowledge of the curriculum for age groups above and below that of your own class is similarly important, together with an understanding of appropriate applications of mathematical matters and processes relevant to other subjects.

3. Thirdly, a command of the subject matter set out in your school's curriculum for your class. This will include science and other foundation subjects, RE, sex and relationships education, PSHE (personal, social and health education) and all other curriculum areas selected by the school. An appreciation of the constituent elements of the subjects involved, expressed in terms of factual information, skills, attitudes and concepts is important.

4. Fourthly, it can be argued that all primary school teachers, not only those teaching younger pupils, should be able to demonstrate a clear understanding of systematic synthetic phonics. There may well be pupils in junior classes who need to revisit some letter/sound correspondences. Such knowledge will also enable you to work productively with pupils entering part way through your school, for example those for whom English is not their first language. The debate about the place of phonics in teaching reading is a complex one, not least because of the irregular nature of English, compared with for example Welsh or Italian, in both of which correspondences are almost invariably regular. Much of the groundwork in this area of the curriculum can be found in Rose (2006), an independent report on the teaching of reading, and extensive advice is contained in Glazzard and Stokoe (2013) and Joliffe et al. (2012).

5. Fifthly, parallel arguments apply to the teaching of mathematics. Williams (2008), an independent report on the teaching of early mathematics, provides the underpinning

for this aspect of the curriculum, with detailed advice to be found in Cotton (2013) and Mooney et al. (2012).

6.   Lastly, you need to appreciate how the formal curriculum, consisting of the planned teaching programme, relates to the wider curriculum of your school, which includes the informal and the hidden curricula (see Chapter 5).

You would be right to think that the subject knowledge requirements implicit in Standard 3 are considerable, although you will have encountered much of the content well before beginning to train as a teacher. During the process of planning, which in most schools is shared among staff members, there is ample opportunity to undertake your own research in order to fill gaps in your own knowledge. However, the acid test of your knowledge arises from contingent teaching events, principally when a pupil asks you a question, or when you are trying to correct a pupil's misconception. These occasions, because of their unpredictability, are impossible to plan for. Inevitably, there will be times when you will not know the answer, although fundamental errors in English and mathematics are not excusable. It is good for pupils to know that teachers don't know everything, and you can turn the situation to an advantage by, for example:

- modelling for pupils ways of finding the information, by using the internet, the library or by asking another person, including other children, and showing your interest in extending your own knowledge;

- setting the class the task of doing some research, including as a homework exercise; and

- planning to cover the issue in a subsequent lesson.

Finally, it is important to remember that knowledge is not finite. New discoveries are continually being made, new knowledge formulated, old knowledge being made to interact with new situations to create fresh interpretations. In addition to your important role in mediating the encounter between your pupils and the existing knowledge embodied in public culture, you are also well placed to show your pupils what it means to participate in the creation of knowledge. You will constantly expect children to create stories, poems, pieces of art, designs, scientific experiments and gymnastic routines. Should you not sometimes undertake these tasks yourself? By doing so, you will convey to your class a great deal about the relevance and importance of the subject matter, and you will enjoy the satisfaction of creating, as well as transmitting, subject knowledge.

Performance of understanding

Thinking about the school in which you work or have recently worked, respond to the prompts after each intended learning outcome, as a means of identifying your knowledge and understanding of the issues covered in the chapter.

- *an appreciation of the nature of subjects and their contribution to human experience and understanding;*

     – Choose three subjects or curriculum areas that you recently taught. How would you express to your class the value and purpose of studying each of them?

– To what extent do you think the three are valuable for their own sake, and in what ways do they have practical applications in the lives of the pupils, now and/or in the future?

- *an awareness of the relationship between subject knowledge and pedagogical subject knowledge;*

  – Reflect on your planning for one area of the curriculum that you recently taught. Analyse how you decided upon particular teaching and learning approaches to enable your pupils to access the subject matter at their own levels.

  – Selecting a different area of the curriculum that you recently taught, identify a key concept covered in your planning. Reflect on how that concept is developed for pupils from the EYFS curriculum, through Key Stages 1 and 2 and on into secondary education.

- *your knowledge of the whole curriculum, and of the place within it of the national curriculum;*

  – Distinguish in the curriculum that you have recently taught between the content drawn from the national curriculum and material from elsewhere.

  – Do you consider that each of the areas that you taught is of equal importance? If not, what reasons do you have for placing them in a hierarchy of importance?

- *an understanding of the knowledge that you need in order to teach the whole curriculum, with particular attention to English and mathematics.*

  – Identify examples from your teaching to illustrate how you promoted high standards of English, in speech, reading and writing, when teaching other areas of the curriculum.

  – Identify opportunities that you took to apply mathematical knowledge and skills appropriately when teaching other areas of the curriculum.

Taking it further

Hansen, A et al. (2012) *Reflective Learning and Teaching in Primary Schools*. London: Sage.

Ofsted (2009) *Improving Primary Teachers' Subject Knowledge across the Curriculum*. (070252). London: Ofsted.

References

Alexander, R, Rose, J and Woodhead, C (1992) *Curriculum Organisation and Classroom Practice in Primary Schools: A Discussion Paper*. London: DES.

Allingham, S (2011) *Transitions in the Early Years*. London: MA Education Ltd.

Birbili, M (2006) Mapping Knowledge: Concept Maps in Early Childhood Education. *Early Childhood Research and Practice*, 8 (2). Available online at www.ecrp.uiuc.edu/v8n2/birbili.html (accessed 10 April 2014).

Bloom, B (1956) *Taxonomy of Educational Objectives: The Classification of Educational Goals, Handbook 1, Cognitive Domain*. New York: David McKay.

Bruner, J S (1960) *The Process of Education*. Cambridge, MA: Harvard University Press.

Callaghan, L J (1976) The 'Ruskin College' Speech. *The Guardian*, 15 October 2001.

Cotton, T (2013) *Understanding and Teaching Primary Mathematics*. London: Pearson Education.

Department for Education (DfE) (2012) *Statutory Framework for the Early Years Foundation Stage*. London: DfE.

Department for Education (DfE) (2013) *The National Curriculum in England: Key Stages 1 and 2 Framework Document*. London: DfE.

Department of Education and Science (DES) (1988) *The Education Reform Act, 1988*. London: DES.

Elliott, L (2011) Overseas Workers Preferred Over 'Unskilled' School Leavers in Jobs Market. *The Guardian*, 23 August 2011.

Ewens, T (2011) The School Community: Being Part of a Wider Professional Environment, in Hansen, A (ed) *Primary Professional Studies*. Exeter: Learning Matters.

Galton, M et al. (2003) *Transfer and Transitions in the Middle Years of Schooling*. (DfES Research Report 443). London: DfES.

Garner, R (2013) British Education in Crisis? Literacy and Numeracy Skills of Young People in UK among Lowest in Developed World. *The Independent*, 8 October 2013.

Glazzard, J and Stokoe, J (2013) *Teaching Systematic Synthetic Phonics and Early English*. Northwich: Critical Publishing.

Her Majesty's Inspectorate (HMI) (1985) *The Curriculum from 5 to 16*. (HMI Series: Curriculum Matters No. 2). London: HMSO.

Joliffe, W et al. (2012) *Teaching Systematic Synthetic Phonics in Primary Schools*. London: Sage.

Kelly, L and Stead, D (2013) *Enhancing Primary Science: Developing Effective Cross-Curricular Links*. Maidenhead: Open University Press.

Lefrançois, G R (1999) *Psychology for Teaching*. Tenth edition. Belmont, CA: Wadsworth.

Mooney, C et al. (2012) *Primary Mathematics: Knowledge and Understanding*. London: Sage.

Rose, J (2006) *Independent Review of the Teaching of Early Reading: Final Report*. (DfES 0201–2006DOC-EN). London: DfES.

Rose, J (2009) *Independent Review of the Primary Curriculum: Final Report*. (DCSF-00499–2009). London: DCSF.

Ryle, G (1949) *The Concept of Mind*. London: Hutchinson.

Sanders, D et al. (2005) *A Study of the Transition from the Foundation Stage to Key Stage One*. (DfES Research Report SSU/2005/FR/013). London: DfES.

Shulman, L S (1986) Those Who Understand: Knowledge Growth in Teaching. *Educational Researcher*, 15 (2): 4–31.

Sutherland, R et al. (2010) *Supporting Learning in the Transition from Primary to Secondary School*. Bristol: University of Bristol.

The Guardian (2001) Towards a National Debate: Full Text of a Speech by Prime Minister James Callaghan at Ruskin College, Oxford, on 18 October 1976. *The Guardian*, 15 October 2001.

Twiselton, S (2006) The Problem with English: The Exploration and Development of Student Teachers' English Subject Knowledge in Primary Classrooms. *Literacy*, 40 (2): 88–96.

White, J (2005) Reassessing 1960s Philosophy of the Curriculum. *London Review of Education*, 3 (2): 131–44.

Whitehead, A N (1950) The Aims of Education, in *The Aims of Education and Other Essays*. Second edition. London: Ernest Benn.

Williams, P (2008) *Independent Review of Mathematics Teaching in Early Years Settings and Primary Schools*. (DCSF 00433–2008BKT-EN). London: DCSF.

4 Well-structured teaching

Learning outcomes

By the end of this chapter you should have developed and clarified:

*   *your ability to use lesson time effectively to promote pupils' knowledge, skills and understanding;*

*   *an appreciation of how to stimulate children's interest in, and love of, learning;*

*   *an awareness of how to plan homework tasks to complement and extend what has been learned at school;*

*   *your capacity to evaluate your teaching, and pupils' learning, in a systematic and constructive way; and*

*   *your ability to contribute to the design and implementation of an engaging curriculum which is broad, balanced and relevant.*

Introduction

The fourth of the Teachers' Standards, entitled 'Plan and teach well structured lessons', appears straightforward and obvious. You would of course be right to think that all your teaching, whether of an individual lesson or a longer-term sequence of lessons, should be thoroughly planned. It may appear that experienced teachers operate with less planning than more recent recruits to the profession, but this judgement probably relates only to the quantity of paperwork that they produce. Seasoned professionals often hold a great deal of information about their pupils' needs and desired learning outcomes in their heads. This enables them to reduce the volume of written plans, but should not be seen as a failure to plan. It does, however, enable them to incorporate a good deal of flexibility into their teaching, whereas a very detailed written plan can easily make a teacher less able – or, perhaps, less willing – to modify the lesson in the light of pupils' responses.

The purposes of planning

Banks (2007) enumerates the benefits of thorough planning as ensuring that you:

- *think carefully about learning objectives, differentiated for groups and individuals;*
- *consider the sequence and timing of each part of a lesson;*
- *can move confidently from stage to stage of the lesson;*
- *prepare materials and resources; and*
- *generate a basis for evaluation and future reference.*

(Banks, 2007, p 3)

These are important characteristics of good teaching. It is easy to fall into the trap of viewing your written planning as an end in itself, rather than as a means to the ends that Banks rightly identifies as important. In the earliest stages of learning to teach, teachers understandably concentrate on what they – rather than the children – are doing, and their plans are consequently biased towards their own performance. A crucial phase in a teacher's development concerns the ability to de-centre, and plan lessons from the standpoint of what the children are intended to learn, and how they will be supported in doing so. As well as thinking about the plan for each lesson, it is vital to consider how the lesson relates to its wider context, for example as part of a sequence of lessons. Briggs' (2011) examination of levels of planning provides a useful introduction to this topic by offering an analysis of the main features of long-, medium- and short-term planning (Briggs, 2011, pp 207–11). These three aspects of planning can readily be related to the concepts of aims, objectives and goals.

A planning timescale

- *Aims* – In educational discourse, the word aim refers to a long-term aspiration. Examples include 'appreciating literature', 'knowing trigonometry' and 'understanding the universe'. Notice how these can never be fully realised, and any assessment of a person's achievement of them could only be inexact. There is always something more that can be learned about literature, trigonometry and the universe.

- *Objectives* – At the opposite extreme, an objective is something that can be attained in the space of a single lesson, for example 'being able to write a rhyming couplet', 'knowing the factors of 24' or 'recalling the names of the planets in the solar system', any of which might be appropriate at upper Key Stage 2. These are obviously very precise, measurable targets.

- *Goals* – Somewhere between aims and objectives come goals, which can be defined as the learning intentions to be assessed after a sequence of lessons. Examples of goals at upper Key Stage 2 might be 'being able to articulate an appreciation of some of Charles Causley's poems', 'knowing and understanding that the sum of the angles in a triangle is always 180°' and 'being able to describe the movement of the Earth, and other planets, relative to the Sun in the solar system'.

These different types of target shape the way in which teachers plan. All are essential. If you focus exclusively on planning single lessons, you will lose sight of the overall destination that you are hoping to reach in that area of the curriculum in, say, half a term. However good each of the lessons, the sequence of lessons will lack coherence and forward thrust. If, on the other hand, you concentrate excessively on your overall plan for the half term, even with carefully designed goals in mind, you will certainly miss some of the key steps that children need to make in their learning, and the resultant gaps in their knowledge will detract from their progress.

It follows that your approach to planning must take account of all three levels. As Briggs makes clear, the long-term plans are drawn up at school level (Briggs, 2011, p 207) and this is a shared responsibility. Planning will obviously be informed by the provisions of the national curriculum, if that is what the school follows, but it will also be rooted in the school's unique circumstances and ethos. For example, a school with mixed-age classes – which includes many larger schools as well as most small ones – will need a different approach from one with single-age classes. Your input will depend on your specific responsibilities in the school. For instance, you may be a subject leader, in which case you are likely to be accountable to the head teacher for long-term planning. But since all teachers are staff members, not just class teachers, all can have a voice in shaping and revising whole school plans. Medium-term planning may be your sole responsibility if yours is the only class in a particular year group. If there are parallel classes, it is usually a shared responsibility for the staff concerned. Short-term planning, at the level of the individual lesson, will be down to you, although teachers in parallel classes often work together at this level, too.

REFLECTIVE TASK

Reflecting on your teaching

»   *Thinking about the school in which you work or have recently worked, identify how the three levels of planning, referred to by Briggs, work in your school from your experience of using its systems and procedures.*

»   *What influence do individual members of staff have on the long-term plans?*

»   *What staffing structure (for example, identified subject or phase leaders) ensures that suitable expertise is matched to the task of planning the overview of each area of the curriculum?*

»   *How does the school facilitate the process of medium-term planning? For instance, how do individual teachers access the expertise of specialist colleagues when translating long-term plans into medium-term programmes for their classes?*

»   *Reflect on how you have drawn on colleagues' experience and strengths for the benefit of your own class when planning.*

>> *Have you also been able to contribute your specialist knowledge to assist a colleague?*

>> *How do you, as a class teacher, ensure that your short-term lesson plans for each subject result in well-progressed sequences of lessons?*

>> *Finally, try to identify one or more occasions when you have modified your medium-term plans as a consequence of reviewing the successes and shortcomings of your lesson plans. Consider the potential benefits and drawbacks of doing this.*

From planning to teaching

Two issues arise when you plan how best to use time during your lessons. The first concerns the duration of a lesson. In many primary schools the day is divided into four lengthy periods, punctuated by morning and afternoon breaks and a lunch break. Apart from these necessary stopping points, the only other limitations on how you allocate your time relate to whole school occasions such as collective worship, activities requiring specific spaces and apparatus, such as PE, and sessions when other staff teach your class. Yet all too often, each lesson expands or contracts to fill the next slot in the day. This may not be the best way to use time. While it is tempting to think of giving each area of the curriculum a 'fair' amount of time, it does not always follow that all subjects need the same length of lesson. For example, some topics may be adequately dealt with in an intensive 30-minute session, while others need to be spread over half a day in order to do them justice. If you find that you have to pad out some sessions, or cut others short because of time pressures, the answer may be to vary the length of time for which you plan.

A second, related, issue concerns the structure of a lesson. It is fashionable to plan:

* an introduction, in which you announce learning objectives, make links to prior learning and give some direct input;

* a main task for the children to undertake;

* and finally a plenary, in which you review what has been learned in the light of the intended outcomes.

While 'beginning, middle and end' is often ideal, it is not inevitable. You will often notice that, during a main task, the children's energy flags and their work loses impetus. Much can be gained by stopping the lesson, dealing with common difficulties, re-teaching where there are shared misconceptions, showcasing examples of good work and progress, then re-launching the task. The fresh impetus can result in better outcomes than would have been obtained by allowing the session to meander to its close.

Planning and teaching: structure and freedom

The question of how 'tight' your planning and teaching should be is an important consideration. It relates closely to your vision of education. Dadds (2002) characterises much classroom practice as a 'hurry along' curriculum (p 173), in which the emphasis is on coverage of the sheer quantity of material, to the detriment of learning. The implication is that teachers tend to pay more attention to the subject matter to be learned than to the developmental needs of the children they teach. The question of balancing curriculum content with pupils' experiences, discussed in Chapter 3, is the key issue here. The touchstone for judging the appropriate balance lies in the advice of Alexander et al. (1992) that the teacher's prime duty is 'to mediate the encounter between pupils' private understandings and the public knowledge embodied in our cultural traditions' (para 64).

In a classic text, Whitehead (1950) reflects on 'The Rhythmic Claims of Freedom and Discipline'. He describes the pupil's mind as a growing organism, and claims that, 'It is not a box to be ruthlessly packed with alien ideas: and, on the other hand, the ordered acquirement of knowledge is the natural food for a developing intelligence' (Whitehead, 1950, p 47). Consequently he makes the case for an education which is both rigorous, in the sense that the teacher presents knowledge for the pupil to learn, and free, in that the teacher gives the pupil scope to process the knowledge. This might take the form of asking questions, investigating different examples of the same principle, and applying the knowledge to a range of circumstances. In short, the pupil should learn why a piece of knowledge is useful, and practise using it.

Whitehead argues persuasively that an education which is over-balanced towards imparting what he calls 'mere knowledge' dulls the pupil's interest. Arousing children's interest entails engaging them in a process of 'shaping questions, of seeking for answers, of devising new experiences, of noticing what happens as the result of new ventures' (Whitehead, 1950, p 50).

If you take Whitehead's vision seriously, you are confronted with a dilemma about the nature of planning. The investigative and experimental work implied by Whitehead's description of 'freedom' possesses an open-ended character. Even with the benefit of much experience, it is impossible fully to predict what questions, discoveries and hypotheses children may arrive at during activities of this kind. You cannot therefore write a plan that sets out in detail what will happen during the lesson. If you give children the freedom to work with the knowledge that you have imparted to them, some of the outcomes are bound to be unexpected. The acid tests of your subject knowledge, your teaching skills and your ability to manage the class arise at times of unplanned interaction. These may take the form of a contingent intervention which you instigate, for example to correct a misconception by explaining or re-teaching. Alternatively a pupil may prompt the exchange with a question. In either event, you are committed to taking risks, because you cannot predict children's questions or misconceptions.

If you are a risk-averse teacher, your reaction may be to eliminate risk by limiting the scope of your teaching to what can be planned in detail. But that restricts your lessons to 'delivering a curriculum', which is exactly what Whitehead criticises. It is the open-ended elements of learning which enable children to engage with knowledge and stimulate their interest and engagement. When planning and teaching any lesson, or sequence of lessons, you consequently need to include spaces in which this investigative type of work can be pursued. Successful negotiation of these parts of the lesson depends on a more general type of planning: the development of a secure subject knowledge, a repertoire of teaching skills appropriate to exploratory learning, and a relationship with your pupils based on a belief that they, with you, are in the business of creating knowledge as well as soaking it up.

To some extent, your readiness to engage in providing your pupils with freedom as well as structure is a matter of confidence and experience. It is also a function of your developing expertise. Alexander (2010, pp 406–36) describes five stages of the development of teacher expertise, and demonstrates that the continuum is a question of professional learning, not just of increasing experience. This holds implications for how you plan your programme of Continuing Professional Development.

REFLECTIVE TASK

Reflecting on your reading

Twiselton, S (2006) The Problem with English: The Exploration and Development of Student Teachers' English Subject Knowledge in Primary Classrooms, *Literacy,* 40 (2): 88–96.

Twiselton's article divides a group of primary trainee teachers into three sub-sets:

* 'task managers', who emphasise the orderly conduct of lessons with little regard for the quality of learning that they foster;

* 'curriculum deliverers', who concentrate more on learning but have a restricted view of teaching as transmission of knowledge; and

* *'concept/skill builders', who encourage pupils to engage with their knowledge to develop their understanding and competence.*

Although conducted with respect to the teaching of English, Twiselton's research has a wider application, as it identifies a developmental continuum in the professional formation of teachers.

» *Reflect on the potential impact of Twiselton's findings on your own vision and practice. What implications can you identify for your approach to planning and teaching?*

Planning and teaching: learning and order

The teachers described by Twiselton as 'task managers' were intent on conducting lessons that were orderly, and gave little thought to the educational quality of the tasks that they set. Doyle (1985) identifies a tension between management and curriculum in the way in which teachers run their classrooms. What happens in the classroom is defined by both the rules for social participation and the demands of academic work, meaning that teachers have to plan for both order and learning. Doyle's overview of research points to the conclusion that, as he puts it, 'Academic work can become swamped by the management function in teaching, and teachers can become preoccupied with getting work accomplished rather than promoting student learning' (Doyle, 1985, p 1).

Accepting that a certain level of orderliness is a prerequisite of successful learning activities, Doyle nevertheless identifies occasions when teachers' focus on maintaining order resulted in a diminution of opportunities for learning, even when the level of student engagement was high. A feature in such circumstances is a tacit negotiating down between pupils and teacher of the academic demands of the task. For example, a task offering a high level of risk and/or ambiguity, and requiring students to hypothesise and investigate, might well give rise to a perceived diminution in order. The pupils might engage in lively discussion, embark on adventurous experimental activities, and generally take control of their own learning to an extent that appeared to question the teacher's management of the classroom. The teacher might respond by reducing the level of challenge, for instance by giving pupils part of the solution to a demanding task, rather than appear to be accepting an apparently disorderly classroom. The consequence is an unspoken agreement whereby the class agrees to co-operate with the teacher, on the understanding that they will not be unduly taxed by the demands of the tasks that are set. These outcomes challenge the commonly held view that tight management enables students to learn the curriculum. On the contrary, tight management can sometimes inhibit and thwart learning.

Doyle's findings take you beyond the topic of planning, into the realms of classroom practice. However, the key to avoiding the trap of the teacher being 'negotiated down' by the class lies in strong planning. Doyle found that teachers who were asked about the academic content of their lessons (Doyle, 1986) were not necessarily adept at defining it in terms of purpose and challenge. This is an important starting point. While it can be useful to accept Doyle's description of teachers as 'circus ringmasters', who are trying to manage a complex and active environment, it is vital to ensure that you are promoting learning, not just order. His analysis of the role of tasks in learning suggests that a balanced programme, in which some but not all tasks exhibit characteristics of risk and/or ambiguity, will best promote learning while maintaining equilibrium. The nature and the level of demand of each of the various tasks that you plan for the class are both important considerations. Your planning should also include making opportunities to explain to your class that, while you are there to help them, there are occasions when you want them to puzzle things out for themselves.

In your planning and teaching you will be well advised to keep learning intentions at the front of your mind, allowing your plans for managing the classroom to be shaped and determined by the demands of the intended learning. Not for nothing are the subjects of the curriculum sometimes called 'disciplines'. Each calls for particular types of behaviour from learners, according to the various skills and activities through which pupils can best access the subject. For example, team sports require plenty of interaction among team members; group work in design and technology calls for discussion, for the use of tools and materials and sometimes noisy experimentation; while writing a poem might well be a solitary, silent activity. It is worth explaining to children why the demands of different subjects mean that you have varying expectations of their behaviour from one lesson to another. You can also promote their metacognitive development by articulating for them the way in which the skills that you teach them are used as tools for manipulating the information that they need to acquire.

REFLECTIVE TASK

Reflecting on your reading

Bennett, T (2014) 'I Know Therefore I Can', *Times Educational Supplement*, 10 January 2014, pp 26–30.

Bennett discusses the tension around whether we should teach knowledge or skills. Pointing out that 'Skills are knowledge in context' (Bennett, 2014, p 27) and that skills need content upon which to operate, he demonstrates that 'The true expert accumulates knowledge in context, with one fact locking arms with its neighbour in a relationship that shines light on both and embraces further content' (Bennett, 2014, p 30). In other words, for knowledge to be coherent rather than a collection of disconnected scraps, learners need to be able to handle it with skill. Practice (in the sense of tackling multiple examples of the same sort of process) is an important factor in embedding learning. Bennett quotes with approval John Holt's comment that, because content changes in a context of rapid innovation, 'we should turn out people who love learning so much and learn so well that they will be able to learn whatever needs to be learned' (Bennett, 2014, p 28).

»   *Reflect on the extent to which your planning and teaching enable pupils to deal with new content skilfully, so that they are able to expand and enrich their prior knowledge. Piaget's concepts of accommodation and assimilation (see Chapter 2) are relevant to this process.*

Planning and learning: independence and learned helplessness

Bennett's article makes a strong case for the promotion of independence in learning as a vital component of a child's education. Accumulating a store of factual information cannot be the sole purpose of schooling, since much of it will become obsolete quite soon. Consequently, learning how to learn must be a prime goal of education. Claxton (2007) clarifies the meaning of 'capacity to learn', quoting with approval Papert's claim that 'We need to produce people who *know how to act when they are faced with situations for which they were not specifically prepared*' (Claxton, 2007, p 115 – Claxton's italicisation). Given a fundamental knowledge base in core content, and a varied repertoire of learning strategies, pupils are ready to reduce their dependence on the teacher as the source of all knowledge.

Doyle's findings about tacit agreement to negotiate down the academic demands of tasks are applicable here, as they should prompt you to maintain the level of challenge that you have judged it appropriate to include in the tasks that you set for your pupils. That can include setting limits on the amount, or the type, of help that you and other adults in the classroom are prepared to offer in a particular lesson. It is important to bear in mind the concept of 'learned helplessness'. The natural inclination of teachers and teaching assistants is to help children. However, this can give rise to circumstances in which children automatically ask for adult help rather than making an attempt to tackle a difficult assignment by themselves. Carr and Claxton (2002) offer a valuable characterisation of some of the learning dispositions worth fostering in pupils as stepping stones to independent learning, together with proposals for assessing the growth of these dispositions.

REFLECTIVE TASK

Reflecting on alternative perspectives

Consider the following contributions from school staff members talking about their school's plans to enable pupils to become more independent in their learning:

Teacher M: *Our head teacher returned from a conference about the deployment of support staff, and told our staff meeting about the DISS Report (Blatchford et al. 2012 – and see Chapter 8 of this book). The report contained evidence that teaching assistants' overall impact on pupil performance was often negative. When we discussed this, one of our TAs commented that the pupils tended to look to her to do things that they might very well be able to do by themselves. 'It's like my own children at home', she said. 'If they think I'll do something for them, they'll not lift a finger. And because time is often tight I give in and do it, whereas I ought to insist and make them do it, even if it takes longer'. We all thought there might be something in this.*

Teacher N: *An issue that we identified was that there is too much material in the curriculum. One reason that we take the easy option and give too much help to children is so that we can cover everything we're supposed to teach. After discussing it, we decided that this issue was so important that we would concentrate on it over the next half term. It was hard to start with, because it caused major disruption in the way in which some children had grown accustomed to working. But now the pupils know that there's no point in giving up without trying. They are also used to the fact that we usually offer indirect types of help first. For example, we may ask a series of questions to prompt their thinking, or we may direct them to a resource that they can use, rather than simply telling them an answer. We're becoming far more discerning about the different types of help that adults can offer.*

Teacher M: *Yes, and we're getting a much clearer vision about the importance of helping children to learn for themselves.*

» *What factors, other than the constraints of time and an overloaded curriculum mentioned in these extracts, might lead teachers and teaching assistants to offer an excessive amount of direct help to children?*

» *Reflect on the demands of external accountability and the expectations of parents. Consider ways of incorporating into your planning and teaching some explicit references to promoting independent learning.*

During lessons in school, there can understandably be a tendency for children who finish first to be given opportunities to undertake independent tasks. This can easily have the consequence that other children seldom or never have the opportunity to work on their own initiative at school. They then miss out on chances to enrich, extend or deepen their knowledge in a way that embeds good habits of private study. To avoid this imbalance, you could usefully review the quantity of content that you expect different groups and individuals to cover during the main part of a lesson, so that all children have time to experience independent learning.

Homework is an obvious example of self-directed learning, and you need to pay careful attention to the activities that you plan for children to do out of school hours. There is much to be said for setting practice tasks as homework, in the light of Bennett's observations, quoted above, about their value in embedding learning and consolidating knowledge. Bearing in mind the concepts of structure and freedom, considered earlier in the chapter, you can also valuably set open-ended tasks which allow children to explore topics for themselves. Homework of this sort lends itself to being followed up in class in ways that allow children to learn from one another, as they can report back orally or in representational form. Another approach to homework is to invite children to set questions, rather than answer those that you have set. Setting questions, across a range of curriculum areas, requires as much content knowledge as answering them. It appeals to pupils as an interesting task, and it can be used subsequently in school, since children's questions can be tackled by some of their peers.

REFLECTIVE TASK

Reflecting on your schooldays

» *Recall and reflect on some of the tasks that you undertook for homework as a school pupil, if possible dating from your time at primary school. What sorts of activity engaged your interest and enthusiasm? Did any seem irrelevant, or set only because it was a requirement that you should do some homework? Think about ways in which your homework was followed up in school. How did teachers acknowledge, value and give feedback on what you had done?*

» *Consider how your responses could usefully inform your own practice in dealing with homework.*

Finally, in the light of Ausubel's (1968) thinking about the crucial importance of beginning with what the learner already knows, you may like to think about the child's context within the community as a valuable resource when undertaking homework. Homework tasks which are carefully thought out, and suitably open-ended, can provide children with opportunities to learn from and alongside other family members, and this process can help to narrow the gap between home and school.

One aspect of homework requiring your careful attention relates to resources. It is important not to assume that all pupils have access at home to resources ranging from books to the internet. Your plans for homework therefore need to be flexible enough to allow all the children to address them.

Evaluating planning, teaching and learning

Judging the success of your teaching, and your pupils' learning, is obviously an important professional activity. Ivett (2007) places evaluation in the context of a cycle of events, following planning and teaching. She accentuates the importance of seeing it as feeding forward into subsequent plans and lessons, and this point is crucial. If you view evaluation primarily as a task to be undertaken because it is a requirement of the school or a university department of education, you are likely to see it as an end in itself. In reality, the insights that you gain from conducting effective evaluation of teaching and learning provide significant material for future planning, alongside the curriculum content due to be addressed in subsequent lessons. Banks (2007, p 23) offers a list of topics that you might consider when reflecting on a lesson or sequence of lessons, while Proctor et al. (1995, p 144) provide a chart of inter-related questions to stimulate your thinking. They valuably sub-divide their questions in a way which compels you to focus on the children's learning as well as your teaching. Some of the possibilities and pitfalls of evaluation are identified in the contributions of experienced mentors quoted in the following reflective tasks:

REFLECTIVE TASKS

Reflecting on your teaching

To what extent is your usual lesson planning pro forma fit for its purpose? Consider the lesson plan that you normally use. In the light of the issues discussed in this chapter, evaluate the blank form, critically considering its strengths and identifying any areas in which it could be improved.

Reflecting on alternative viewpoints

Mentors attending a workshop on Teacher Education were each asked to describe and comment on their experiences of running tutorials in their schools for trainee teachers, with a focus on lesson evaluation. What can you learn from their reflections?

Mentor J: *My trainee, James, wrote a long and very detailed evaluation of a history lesson, but it contained no references to children. Instead, he had written about how he felt the lesson had gone, his timekeeping, the extent to which he had covered the subject matter, how well he had controlled the class and how difficult he found it to write freehand on the whiteboard. I appreciate that he is at an early stage in his training, so I have suggested two activities to help him to focus his evaluations on learning, rather than teaching. First, he is going to observe one group of children during a lesson taught by his class teacher and evaluate what they have learned during the lesson. After that, he will evaluate one of his own lessons, but every statement must be primarily about children.*

Mentor K: *Ursula, my trainee, seems to equate evaluation with self-criticism. She only mentioned things that she thought had gone wrong, and completely ignored several promising aspects of her work with the class. When we discussed the lesson, she was fully aware that most of the children had learned what she had intended, but said she thought there was no point in mentioning that. Next time, I have asked her to produce an evaluation identifying one strong point, on which she can build further improvement, and one difficulty that she needs to address.*

Mentor L: *We have two trainees at our school, and they're chalk and cheese. Shainaz is ultra-conscientious, and she wrote a long evaluation covering almost every aspect of the lesson. Her comments were mostly perceptive, but there was just too much to consider. Ambrose, on the other hand, is a minimalist. His evaluation consisted of notes scribbled on his lesson plan, most of which were illegible, and he found it hard to make sense of them himself. I got the two trainees to comment on each other's evaluations. Ambrose suggested that Shainaz needed to choose just one or two things to carry forward to her next plan. Shainaz, to my surprise, said she thought that annotating your lesson plan was a great idea. She thought it would be good to indicate, by a letter or number on the plan, the aspect of the lesson that needed consideration, then to write a short footnote about each. They are both going to try that approach next time.*

The teacher's role in designing the curriculum

Prior to the national debate (see Chapter 3) leading to the introduction of a national curriculum, teachers often had a great deal of freedom to design the curriculum for their schools, and for their individual classes. While the names of subjects have changed little for over a century, apart from the addition of technologies, what was taught could vary widely from school to school, as could the teaching and learning methods employed. The argument for greater standardisation was compelling, but teachers' early experience of working with a nationally prescribed curriculum in the late 1980s suggested that the pendulum had swung too far. From having too much control over the curriculum, teachers now perceived themselves to have little or none, and many saw themselves as relegated to the status of 'curriculum deliverers', to use Twiselton's term. Periodic revisions to the national curriculum since then have been designed to address concerns about over-prescription and excessive content.

Growing numbers of primary schools are no longer bound by the requirements of the national curriculum, and in those for which it remains compulsory the 2014 version represents a further lessening of centralised direction. Detailed provision is set out for English, mathematics, science and computer science, but guidance for the foundation subjects is brief, and leaves great scope for teachers to flesh out the whole formal curriculum.

A teacher's duty 'to mediate the encounter between pupils' private understandings and the public knowledge embodied in our cultural traditions' (Alexander et al., 1992, para 64) means that teachers need enough freedom to relate curricula to the knowledge, culture and interests that children bring with them to school. No child should feel excluded from his or her curriculum, yet it can be argued that an over-centralised national curriculum has had the effect of excluding or marginalising certain groups. Smith (2006) claims that, although the national curriculum was promoted as an entitlement curriculum for all children, there are instances in which, 'Frustration in finding it difficult to cope with the curriculum, or in understanding its relevance, leads to exclusion through withdrawal and avoidance strategies, truancy or enforced exclusion as a result of disaffection and anti-social behaviour' (Smith, 2006, p 147).

When working with your colleagues to design your school's curriculum, you might reflect on the following questions.

*   What is the range of experiences and understandings that our pupils bring with them from their homes and communities?

*   What strengths do we have among the staff of the school that might underpin distinctive aspects of the curriculum?

*   What specialist interests and enthusiasms are there among members of staff and the wider community that they might contribute?

*   To what extent might children's views and interests be sought and addressed when planning the programme?

*   What resources, human and material, are there in the school's locality that can be capitalised upon?

*   What opportunities can be identified to widen the children's experience, for example through educational visits, outdoor and adventurous activities and links with other organisations?

*   What contributions to the breadth of the curriculum can be made by the arts, humanities and technologies?

*   How can knowledge gained in the core subjects be employed in a variety of curricular contexts to show its application and relevance?

*   How do we define what we mean by a balanced curriculum?

*   How do we ensure that the curriculum that we design both includes and challenges all our pupils?

There is a sense in which it was never going to be possible to define the curriculum by writing it down, as the architects of the Education Reform Act (DES, 1988) tried to do. A curriculum is organic, developing in response to the changing needs of society and the varying educational needs of the pupils. In Chapter 3 it was argued that attention had often been paid to the curriculum at the expense of a consideration of educational aims. Consequently, the questions listed above need to be seen in the light of the school's overall vision for its pupils. Fostering 'the spiritual, moral, cultural, mental and physical development of the children at the school' (DES, 1988) is a vast ambition. The curriculum is a means to that end.

Pring's (1996) notion of 'vocationalised education' offers a valuable organising principle, helping teachers to relate their school's curriculum to their wider responsibility to promote children's all-round development. He advocates a synthesis between a liberal education, drawing on the value of knowledge for its own sake, and a vocational training which prepares pupils for adult life. Pring's model combines knowledge with skill, theory with practice. The implication of his vision is that the education that a school offers should bring together 'the qualities and capacities, the skills and the understandings, which enable all people to live valuable, useful and distinctively human lives' (Pring, 1996, p 114).

All of which might make you think that you should be designing an education, not just a curriculum.

Performance of understanding

Thinking about the school in which you work or have recently worked, respond to the prompts after each intended learning outcome, as a means of identifying your knowledge and understanding of the issues covered in the chapter.

- *your ability to use lesson time effectively to promote pupils' knowledge, skills and understanding;*

    - Identify in your planning some examples of lessons exhibiting a good balance between structure (time controlled by you) and freedom (time in which children could make their individual responses to the topic being studied).

    - With reference to a short sequence of lessons in a subject of your choice, show how you have ensured that your emphasis has been on learning, rather than primarily on managing the class.

- *an appreciation of how to stimulate children's interest in, and love of, learning;*

    - Demonstrate, with examples, how you have enabled children to learn how to learn, and to become more independent in their learning.

    - Recall an occasion when pupils' enthusiasm for something that they were learning about led them to want to learn more. How were you able to stimulate that enthusiasm, and how could you capitalise on that in other areas of the curriculum?

- *an awareness of how to plan homework tasks to complement and extend what has been learned at school;*

    - Identify two or three homework tasks that you have set, and articulate their associated learning intentions. What was the balance between closed (determined by you) and open (determined by the children) outcomes in these activities?

    - How have you been able to use homework tasks to narrow the gap between home and school by providing opportunities for children to learn from and alongside other family members?

- *your capacity to evaluate your teaching, and pupils' learning, in a systematic and constructive way;*

    - Explain how you select the topics that you wish to analyse in a lesson evaluation. Find an example illustrating how you remedied a problem that you identified during an evaluation, and another showing how a strength that you identified became the basis for further enhancement of teaching and learning.

–   What evidence can you produce to show that you made significant changes in a medium-term plan as a result of evaluations that you undertook early in the programme of work?

• *your ability to contribute to the design and implementation of an engaging curriculum which is broad, balanced and relevant.*

–   Identify a personal skill or enthusiasm that you possess and state how you could use it to enrich the curriculum.

–   How have you been able to draw upon your knowledge of your pupils' home and community backgrounds to tailor the curriculum so that it helps to bridge the gap between home and school?

Taking it further

Eaude, T (2012) *How do Expert Classteachers Really Work?* Northwich: Critical Publishing.

Pring, R (1996) Values and Education Policy, in Halstead, J M and Taylor, M J (eds) *Values in Education and Education in Values*. Abing: Falmer Press.

References

Alexander, R (ed) (2010) *Children, Their World, Their Education: Final Report and Recommendations of the Cambridge Primary Review*. Abingdon: Routledge.

Alexander, R, Rose, J and Woodhead, C (1992) *Curriculum Organisation and Classroom Practice in Primary Schools: A Discussion Paper*. London: DES.

Ausubel, D P (1968) *Educational Psychology: A Cognitive View*. New York: Holt, Rinehart and Winston.

Banks, P (2007) Planning for Excellence and Enjoyment, in Jacques, K and Hyland, R (eds) *Professional Studies: Primary and Early Years*. Third edition, Exeter: Learning Matters.

Bennett, T (2014) I Know Therefore I Can. *Times Educational Supplement*, 10 January 2014, pp 26–30.

Blatchford, P, Russell, A and Webster, R (2012) *Reassessing the Impact of Teaching Assistants*. Abingdon: Routledge.

Briggs, M (2011) Planning, in Hansen, A (ed) *Primary Professional Studies*. Exeter: Learning Matters.

Carr, M and Claxton, G (2002) Tracking the Development of Learning Dispositions. *Assessment in Education: Principles, Policy and Practice*, 9 (1), 9–37.

Claxton, G (2007) Expanding Young People's Capacity to Learn. *British Journal of Educational Studies*, 55 (2), 115–34.

Dadds, M (2002) The 'Hurry-Along' Curriculum, in Pollard, A (ed) *Readings for Reflective Teaching*. London: Continuum.

Department of Education and Science (DES) (1988) *The Education Reform Act, 1988*. London: DES.

Doyle, W (1985) Classroom Management and the Curriculum: A Strategic Research Site. *R and D Report 6162*. Austin, TX: University of Texas.

Doyle, W (1986) Content Representation in Teachers' Definitions of Academic Work. *Journal of Curriculum Studies*, 18 (4): 365–79. Available online at www.files.eric.ed.gov/fulltext/ED264222.pdf (accessed 13 January 2014).

Ivett, N (2007) Planning for all Abilities: Inclusion and Differentiation, in Jacques, K and Hyland, R (eds) *Professional Studies: Primary and Early Years*. Third edition. Exeter: Learning Matters.

Pring, R (1996) Values and Education Policy, in Halstead, J M and Taylor, M J (eds) *Values in Education and Education in Values*. London: Falmer Press.

Proctor, A, Entwistle, M, Judge, B and McKenzie-Murdoch, S (1995) *Learning to Teach in the Primary Classroom*. London: Routledge.

Smith, C (2006) From Special Needs to Inclusive Education, in Sharp, J, Ward, S and Hankin, L, *Education Studies: An Issues-Based Approach*. Exeter: Learning Matters.

Twiselton, S (2006) The Problem with English: The Exploration and Development of Student Teachers' English Subject Knowledge in Primary Classrooms, *Literacy*, 40 (2): 88–96.

Whitehead, A N (1950) The Rhythmic Claims of Freedom and Discipline, in *The Aims of Education and Other Essays*. Second edition. London: Ernest Benn.

5 Meeting the needs of all pupils

Learning outcomes

By the end of this chapter you should have developed and clarified:

- *your knowledge of how and when to use a variety of ways of differentiating teaching;*

- *an awareness of factors that may inhibit pupils' ability to learn, and an enhanced capacity to overcome these;*

- *an understanding of pupils' physical, social and intellectual development, and an ability to adapt your teaching to cater for pupils' developmental needs as learners;*

- *your appreciation of the needs of all pupils, especially those with special educational needs, those of high ability, those with English as an additional language, and those with disabilities; and*

- *your ability to use and evaluate distinctive teaching approaches to engage and support all learners.*

Introduction

It is self-evident that the children in your class are all unique persons, and the notion that children receive individual attention from their teachers is popular with parents, especially when they are selecting schools for their offspring to attend. Nevertheless, whole-class teaching conveys many benefits. Treating the pupils as one group gives them experience of belonging to a community. Focusing on chosen curricular topics provides opportunities for children to share their knowledge and interests with one another. Adopting and maintaining protocols for behaviour offers a chance to promote shared values, supports cohesion within the group and provides important lessons for life. That said, it is also important that you develop your knowledge of the widely differing characteristics, abilities and aptitudes of each of the children in your class, so that you can adapt your teaching to respond to their differing needs and circumstances.

The diversity within your classroom will include many, and possibly all, of these:

- girls and boys;
- different ages;
- differences in family composition, including looked after children;
- different ethnic groups;
- differences in prior attainment;
- children with special educational needs;
- children of high ability;
- children with disabilities;
- left handers and right handers;
- different attitudes to school and schooling;
- differences in social class;
- cultural and religious differences;
- different points on the continuum of family poverty and affluence;
- children with a variety of linguistic backgrounds;
- travellers;
- asylum seekers and refugees.

REFLECTIVE TASK

Reflecting on your teaching

»   *Thinking about the class that you teach, or have recently taught, use the bulleted points above to help you to reflect on the characteristics of each child in the class. Notice that most of the items in the list are fixed and unchanging.*

»   *Reflect on other factors that may impact on the children you teach. Can you add to the following list?*

- temporary illness;
- lengthy absence from school for whatever reason;
- birth of a sibling;
- a house move;
- changes in friendship patterns.

When you review your findings, and appreciate the diversity in your class, your first reaction may be to plan individualised lessons for all your pupils, adopting a one-to-one approach. Apart from being totally impracticable, this would also deny your children the benefits of being a class member. You therefore need to find a solution that allows all children to access learning in your classroom while simultaneously belonging to your class. This involves compromise; it also requires regular review.

While your class is definitely not homogeneous in terms of its membership, your school will be endeavouring to engender a sense of oneness among its pupils. An outward manifestation of this is any uniform, badge or sports kit that pupils may wear. Less tangible, but arguably more significant, are the qualities associated with the school ethos. These need to be reflected in your classroom, since they constitute the set of values espoused and promoted by the school. A well-considered ethos, based on clear beliefs and values and expressed through a vision statement, can support the creation of a unified organisation, irrespective of the diversity of its membership. Arguably, the existence and realisation of such an ethos is essential in creating a robust framework within which diversity can be acknowledged, valued and provided for.

Including all pupils?

The concept of inclusion, as used in the education service, is very wide:

> *Educational inclusion is more than a concern about any one group of pupils. Its scope is broad. It is about equal opportunities for all pupils, whatever their age, gender, ethnicity, attainment and background.*
>
> (Ofsted, 2000, p 4)

The national curriculum, from its inception in 1988, was promoted as an entitlement curriculum for all children. Glazzard (2011) traces a long-running argument that there is a fundamental incompatibility in the relationship between the standards agenda and the inclusion agenda (Glazzard, 2011, p 65f). He cites Lloyd's (2008) critique in which she claims that recent policy and practice have focused on normalising individuals and groups, whereas a truly inclusive approach would denormalise 'institutions, systems and rules which comprise education and schooling' (Lloyd, 2008, p 228). Smith (2006) concurs, claiming that

> *Not until school effectiveness is measured only in terms of value-addedness, where success is calculated on how far individuals have progressed from a base-line assessment, will these exclusionary pressures be overcome.*
>
> (Smith, 2006, p 148)

There can be little doubt that it is fruitless to suppose that a narrowly defined curriculum and precise expectations of output measures could be consistent with a truly inclusive vision of education. Indeed, they are likely to bring about the exclusion, even alienation, of those who find the curriculum irrelevant and the expected outcomes a pipedream.

The current debate about targets and levels (see Chapter 1) appears to be heading in the direction recommended by Smith. This would be welcome news to teachers whose pupils may have made significant progress, but from a low starting point from which they were unlikely to meet the nationally expected levels.

Pupils with special educational needs

The tension between standards and inclusion as focal points in education policy poses particular issues for children with special educational needs (SEN). Ainscow's (2007) definition sees inclusion in broad terms as a concept which aims to eliminate social exclusion. However, current public policies are based on the notion that a common curriculum and a single set of norm-related performance indicators are appropriate for all learners. In that view, the key to working with pupils with SEN is to provide added support and adaptations so that they can 'catch up', rather than identifying suitable challenges for the learners, whatever their starting points. A policy underpinned by an inspection and testing regime and linked to published league tables has had, as Smith asserts, 'an adverse effect on the willingness of mainstream schools to include those who would find it difficult to achieve' (Smith, 2006, p 145). Institutional readiness by schools to be inclusive has to be matched by positive attitudes from teachers. They in turn are subject to clashes of values when pressed on the one hand to welcome all learners and on the other to deliver top results in national assessments.

REFLECTIVE TASK

Reflecting on your reading

Glazzard, J (2011) Including all Learners, in Hansen, A (ed) *Primary Professional Studies*. Exeter: Learning Matters.

Read the extended case study provided by Glazzard on pages 76–78 of this chapter. Reflect on the characteristics of the two teachers, 'Sally' and 'Chris', who work with 'Sam', a child with SEN.

Cole's research among parents of children with SEN, summarised on p 77 by Glazzard, indicates that their overriding concern was that their child should be wanted. Note, too, the claim that 'Sam's case study illustrates that children with autism are capable of internalising negative teacher attitudes and this can affect their behaviour' (p 77).

»   *To what extent do you agree with Glazzard's comment that the key difference between the two teachers was that Sally wanted to teach Sam, whereas Chris was reluctant?*

Glazzard's conclusion (p 78) is that 'there is clearly a need for some practitioners to reflect on their own values in relation to the education of learners with special educational needs and until all teachers accept their shared responsibility for the education of all children, genuine inclusion will remain problematic'.

»   *To what extent do you find this judgement challenging in terms of your own thinking and beliefs?*

The SEN Code of Practice (DfES, 2001), due to be revised for September 2014, is itself a revision of an earlier code (DfEE, 1994), which established the principle that all schools and all teachers are responsible for the education of all children, adapting provision where necessary to meet pupils' needs (Mittler, 2000). Currently, the code identifies four areas of SEN:

1. communication and interaction;

2. cognition and learning;

3. behavioural, emotional and social development;

4. sensory and/or physical.

Different degrees of need are reflected in three stages of provision:

1. School Action, where provision is made within the school, supported by the SENDCO (SEN and Disabilities Co-ordinator);

2. School Action Plus, where external agencies such as Educational Psychology are involved;

3. Provision covered by a Statement of Needs.

The emphasis at every level, and in all areas, of SEN is on teamwork. Class teachers are supported throughout by SENDCos, and often have additional staffing in the form of teaching assistants (TAs). However, as both Glazzard and Smith emphasise, the crucial factor in successfully including all pupils in the work of the class lies in the readiness of the teacher to want to teach each pupil.

It is natural for teachers to think that they ought to be prepared during their initial training for teaching across all the areas of SEN. However, on reflection you will appreciate that the range of knowledge assumed by such an aspiration would be immense, so that at best you would only scrape the surface of issues in a tokenistic way. Good texts are available (for example, Goepel et al., 2014; Frederickson and Cline, 2009) to provide a thorough outline of all areas of SEN, and you may find it best to access detailed knowledge on a need-to-know basis, when preparing to teach children identified as having SEN. As Eaude (2012) explains, teachers – and members of other professions – develop their expertise through case knowledge. This means that you remember earlier dealings with pupils who demonstrate specific characteristics, and use your experience to puzzle out ways of working with similar cases later on. Examples are given in the following reflective task:

REFLECTIVE TASK

Reflecting on alternative viewpoints

Consider the contributions of three teachers, asked to recount how they had developed their knowledge of working with pupils with SEN or disabilities. Notice the way in which they make use of case knowledge and engage in experimental approaches.

Teacher T: *Early in my career I taught Paul, identified as on the autistic spectrum, probably exhibiting Asperger's syndrome. With good support from the head teacher and other colleagues I found out about this, partly through reading articles, but mostly by careful observation. A key issue was his lack of awareness of how his behaviour affected others, both children and adults. Following the head's advice, I made a point of giving Paul direct instruction about what to do in different circumstances, especially when he was facing something unfamiliar. This seemed to work quite well. A few years later I taught Reuben, and realised that his situation was similar to Paul's, except that his behaviour was significantly more disruptive. I did some more research about Asperger's, and discovered Carol Gray's work on social stories (eg Gray and White, 2002). My TA and I focused on creating social stories for Reuben and he gradually gained a repertoire of scenarios that he referred to when embarking on particular tasks. We had occasional meetings with his parents, and it was very useful to discuss the sorts of situations at home as well as school that presented Reuben with difficulties. They tried a social stories approach at home and said it helped to depersonalise issues, so that they didn't always feel they were getting at Reuben. Conforming to conventional norms, learned by rote, works for Reuben, whereas sensing that his actions may be upsetting others is not something that he can do.*

Teacher U: *In my probationary year I taught Andy, who was a wheelchair user. His Occupational Therapist visited the school, and pointed out to me that, because he had to sit some way back from the table, the circles in his maths book looked like ellipses to him. It was a simple lesson for me to learn, but since then I've made use of an artist's drawing board, that can be set at an angle, to help children with a variety of disabilities to see a bird's eye view of their work.*

Teacher V: *In my many years of teaching I have met plenty of children identified as having dyslexia. The main point that I would make is that no two cases are the same. There is a range of different aspects of language learning covered by the description, and no-one could write a text book with a 'painting by numbers' approach to teaching pupils with dyslexia. Looking back, I remember teaching Amanda, who found it hard to relate the letters on the page to their sounds in spoken English. Linking reading with writing was helpful. Once Amanda could spell a word, she could usually read it, so her reading books were based on stories that she had written. More recently I have also experimented with different fonts and with coloured overlays – my optician was very helpful with that. In the case of Jagdeep, whom I taught a few years ago, the ideas of right and left, up and down were problematic. There were lots of reversals in his writing and his co-ordination was poor. I became interested in the concept of cross-laterality, as it seemed that Jagdeep was not consistently right handed or left handed. With the aid of a book about dyspraxia (Portwood, 2007) I developed sequences of activities, moving from gross motor skills to finer ones, concentrating on hand–eye co-ordination and on establishing a left to right orientation. Who would have thought that there might be a correlation between your ability to catch a ball and the quality of your handwriting? Over the years I've built up a repertoire of activities and used them on a trial-and-error basis. It's always been useful when we've met as a staff team to share ideas and tips, and to agree on a common strategy, so that children experience consistency of approach from different adults. And above all, I've found it invaluable to talk with children about what they find hard and which approaches are helpful.*

It is clear from the teachers' accounts that their professional expertise is a matter of constant reflection, characterised at its best by:

- close observation of the pupils;

- an accumulation of case knowledge resulting in a repertoire of approaches;

- teamwork among staff and the involvement of parents;

- making use of scholarly articles and books as a source of information;

- a willingness to experiment, using a trial-and-error approach;

- drawing on experience and expertise from other sources;

- talking with children about their learning and being responsive to their suggestions.

If you look again at those seven bullet points, you find nothing in the list that is specifically about SEN. You might describe them as general principles of good teaching. They are, however, particularly relevant to the notion that you can and should adapt your teaching to suit the needs of your pupils, irrespective of whether they have SEN or specific learning difficulties.

Another significant factor arising from the teachers' narratives is the individuality of the pupils under consideration. It is part of your professional responsibility as a teacher to adapt your teaching to the best interests of your pupils, even if what you do runs counter to prevailing orthodoxies and government prescriptions. Teacher V's comments about his work with Amanda indicate that for her, as for many children with dyslexia, the systematic teaching of synthetic phonics is of little help in learning to read, because they find it hard to reconcile what they are taught about sounds with the fact that very many words in English are irregular. Although synthetic phonics is an invaluable part of learning to read for a majority of children, Teacher V has used his professional experience and judgement in deciding to use other methods with Amanda. He knows that if he persists with synthetic phonics he will increase the level of frustration felt by Amanda and pupils like her. It takes a degree of moral and professional courage to opt out of complying with pedagogical approaches that are portrayed as essential. You should only do so when you can fully explain why you have decided to change your methods, and can demonstrate that your preferred approach is more likely to bear fruit.

Children's diverse backgrounds

Much of the section about SEN can be generalised, making it applicable to all teaching. The seven bullet points above offer a good starting point for your consideration of children's varied backgrounds.

Lloyd's critique of an approach that seeks to normalise individuals and groups may help you to reflect on your personal reaction to diversity. If faced by a class drawn from different ethnic, cultural, religious and linguistic groups, is your first thought that this is a problem? If so, think again. Certainly the class will present you with professional challenges, as you seek to adapt your teaching so that it matches your pupils' learning needs. But a problem? The class described above is actually little different from any class in any school. A class in a mono-cultural part of the country will contain just as many differences. Viewed against the checklist at the beginning of this chapter, a whole host of differences is evident in any classroom. The diversity in the mono-cultural school may consist of:

- boys and girls;

- left and right handers;

- older and younger;

- shorter and taller;

- poorer and richer;

- urban and rural;

- having siblings or being an only child;

- living with one, both or no parents.

This reflects the fact that all children are unique and deserving of your individual consideration, not just those in a class where ethnic and linguistic diversity makes differences more immediately apparent.

There are some benefits, but many drawbacks, in treating all the children in a group as a whole class. Knowing that six children who speak English as an additional language (EAL) have Urdu as their first language may be helpful, for example if an Urdu-speaking staff member can assist their learning. However the concept of 'labelling' has many negative connotations. Hassan (2006) draws attention to the damage done by generalisations and stereotyping when considering ethnic groups. Like Smith, she pinpoints the tension between an emphasis on published results and an inclusive philosophy. Aggregated test results have regularly placed African-Caribbean pupils, especially boys, in lower positions than their white and Asian peers. Reports over the past 40 years have reached the same conclusions as Swann (DES, 1985), who found that, 'the stereotypes teachers tend to have of West Indian children are often particular, and generally negative, expectations of academic performance' (DES, 1985, p 236).

Careful consideration of the circumstances should lead you to ask searching questions, for example:

- Are factors other than ethnicity involved?

- Are socio-economic considerations pertinent?

- What is the range of attainment of African-Caribbean children?

- Is there typically a mismatch between what African-Caribbean children and their parents expect from their schooling and what the education system delivers?

It is noticeable that some ethnic minority pupils, for example from Indian and Chinese backgrounds, are likely to score highly in published test results, while other Asian pupils have lower scores. Analysis of the data suggests that socio-economic circumstances, coupled with parental aspirations linked to their types of employment, correlate with the educational outcomes. This suggests that pupils tend to achieve highly when their schooling matches their expectations and their parents' aspirations. A mismatch in these aspects tends to be predictive of lower outcomes.

Lloyd's (2008) discussion of normalisation applies here with respect to the culture of schooling. The teachers' expectations criticised by Swann arise from a belief that the pupils should fit into the culture of the school. An opposing view is that it is the responsibility of the school to make its provision accessible to its pupils. Eaude's (2012) remarks about the value of basing education on what children bring with them into school (Eaude, 2012, p 11), discussed in Chapter 1, is particularly relevant, as it is a prime way in which you can adapt your teaching to the needs of your pupils. The views of a head teacher, reported in the following task, are pertinent.

REFLECTIVE TASK

Reflecting on alternative viewpoints

Consider the views of this head teacher, who leads a large primary school which includes pupils from a number of ethnic minority groups:

Head teacher F: *For me and my staff it is vitally important not to conceive of teaching as filling empty vessels. If we think of the curriculum only as something that we are expected to deliver to the children, there is a risk that they will see school as divorced from their general experience of life. So we do our best to find out about our pupils and their backgrounds, so that we can build at least some of the curriculum upon what is already familiar to them. For example, humanities projects can be based on a local study which includes geographical and historical features, with links to religion and the arts. Children love talking about topics from their own experience, and to have those contributions valued at school affirms their personal dignity and worth. We take the same approach in the arts and PE. For example, some of our African-Caribbean children taught their class some playground games that their grandparents had recalled. The activities were accompanied with songs and rhymes. Those children felt ten feet tall to have their contributions included in that way.*

At the same time, we also think it's vital to ensure that all our pupils have a good grounding in a common core of knowledge and skills. A command of English is central, together with maths, science and computer science. We teach these systematically and also practise them in contexts such as the humanities projects that I mentioned. Underpinning my comments is a philosophy which proclaims that we should honour what each child brings to school (such as their language, culture, religion, interests and values), and also prepare each child to play a full part in society at large. You don't achieve community cohesion by pretending that diversity doesn't exist, but by linking diversity to a common spine of knowledge and experience.

Reflect on the head teacher's philosophy.

» *To what extent do you agree with it? Why? If your views differ, try to pin down a rationale for your own opinions.*

» *Is there anything in the head teacher's account that might not be relevant to any school?*

Notice how the head teacher's approach precisely exemplifies the fundamental recommendation of the 'Three Wise Men' report, referred to in Chapter 3, that the teacher's key role is to mediate the encounter between pupils' personal ideas and those embodied in public discourse.

The head teacher's emphasis on the importance of core English draws attention to the particular learning needs of those for whom English is an additional language. There is no shortage of advice on how to support such children in English lessons and across the whole curriculum. Cortazzi and Lixian (2007) outline a systematic strategy for working with narrative (fiction and non-fiction), using keywords and story maps applicable to both oral and written English. Gardner's (2006) article explores the value of dual language texts, and Mistry and Sood (2012) provide a valuable evaluatory framework.

As argued earlier in this chapter, a key approach is to identify the rich range of experiences that children bring with them into the classroom, and Safford and Drury (2013) argue that multilingualism is to be seen as a pedagogical resource rather than a problem.

The informal and hidden curricula

The emphasis so far in this section has been on the value of differentiating the formal curriculum so as to include all learners. The informal and hidden curricula can also help or hinder the process. The informal curriculum refers to the non-compulsory elements of a school's provision. This includes lunchtime or after-school clubs and opportunities to undertake out-of-hours trips including residential opportunities. The tenor of pupil/teacher relationships on these occasions is often very different from usual, and you would not be the first teacher to discover that an extra-curricular link with a child transformed the way in which you could work with him or her on a normal school day. That factor alone might convince you of the value of giving a little of your valuable time to engage in extra-curricular activities. Playground duty at break or lunchtime is another occasion when you interact with children informally, and you may well find yourself latched onto by individual children or small groups with information that they wish to share with a sympathetic adult. These exchanges can be significant, occasionally for reasons to do with child protection (see Chapter 9), but more often because they can provide a real insight into the lives of children outside school and the consequent impact on their learning.

The hidden curriculum refers especially to the quality of the relationships that children experience in school, and the values promoted intentionally or unintentionally by their teachers and other staff members. It is important that you are aware of the climate of values that you are creating, and to consider the effect of your own attitudes and beliefs upon the class.

REFLECTIVE TASK

Reflecting on your schooldays

Thinking about some of the teachers who taught you at primary school, identify a few examples related to the notion of the hidden curriculum.

» *Was there a teacher who conveyed a sense that s/he valued all pupils equally, or another who seemed to favour some pupils over others?*

» *Were some pupils 'approved of' and others 'disapproved of'?*

» *Which teachers made you feel that they really wanted to teach you, and how did this affect you and your attitudes towards particular lessons or school in general?*

Ewens (2007) offers a list of questions designed to help teachers to audit the impact that their values may be making on their classes. These vary from, 'Do you only put the very best work on display, or do you ensure that every child has some of his/her work valued in this way?' to 'Do you, however inadvertently, indicate some tasks as fit for girls and others for boys? If children express such judgements, do you challenge and discuss them, or ignore them?' (Ewens, 2007, p 144).

Hyland (2007) points out that

> Schools are not just concerned that children should achieve in academic terms; they are also concerned with the promotion of values for all children....There is also a concern that schools should explicitly combat racist attitudes and prejudices.
> (Hyland, 2007, p 156f)

While this statement will be overtly addressed in your school's policies and procedures, it has implications for the way in which you operate as a teacher. Do you in fact challenge racist attitudes and prejudices if they arise in your classroom or in the playground? If so, how do you do so without damaging your relationship with the children who express those attitudes and prejudices? After all, they are quite likely to be reflecting what they hear and see in the wider community. Distinguishing your disapproval of certain behaviours from your regard for the perpetrators is hard. Ensuring that you display the same level of moral sophistication in unguarded moments is doubly difficult. To add to the demand upon your personal values and professional conduct, you need to bear in mind Hassan's objection to the notion of tolerance:

> Tolerance means to put up with, perhaps reluctantly. It means to endure or permit grudgingly. It is not about acceptance, understanding and most significantly it is not about equality.
> (Hassan, 2006, p 137)

In the light of this challenging statement, it is clear that congruence between your words, your deeds and the attitudes that you display is absolutely crucial.

Differentiation and match

Making sure that your teaching engages all your pupils in a way that advances their learning is a formidable challenge, in view of the range of diversity previously identified. Three main approaches to differentiation are usually identified:

1. differentiation by task, in which different tasks are set for pupils of different abilities;

2. differentiation by outcome, in which the tasks set can be completed at different levels;

3. differentiation by support, in which the type and level of support offered to different pupils is varied.

An example of differentiation by task is a maths lesson about multiplication, in which one group receives a task involving double-digit numbers, another works with single-digit numbers and a third manipulates structured apparatus to support their learning of the basic concept.

Writing a piece of fiction can lend itself to differentiation by outcome, since the outcomes can vary by length, complexity and vocabulary, with different expectations set for different individuals and groups.

Differentiated support could take the form of helping one group to read the instructions before undertaking a science experiment, while expecting another group to work independently. A third group might be supported by being challenged to extend their thinking about the possible interpretation of the data resulting from the experiment. For any of the groups, the availability of apparatus and extra data might be appropriate.

Notice how your planning of all three types of differentiation is crucially related to assessment.

Grouping the class for the maths activity requires you to know the levels of understanding and skill of the pupils, so that you are aware of which children are ready to be challenged with the double-digit numbers, which the single-digit task and which have yet to grasp the fundamental concept of multiplication so that they need to undertake the practical task with structured apparatus.

The open-ended task in English sounds easier to set, since all the children can tackle it, at their own levels. However, you will certainly have differing expectations of your pupils. The source of these expectations ought to be your assessment of their previous work, which you should have marked in a way that offers individual guidance for future writing.

In the science task, decisions about allocating extra support should have a clear rationale. You may be adopting Vygotsky's advocacy of differentiated scaffolding to enable pupils to take the next steps in their learning (see Chapter 2). If so, you need a clear idea of which children need what support. You must also think carefully about how you allocate that support. The findings of the DISS report (Blatchford et al., 2012 – see Chapter 8) draw attention to the fact that extra adult help can sometimes lead to a reduction in outcomes, rather than the expected benefits. You must therefore be careful about briefing TAs and volunteers, and you should ensure that the learning of the lower ability groups is not always left to them, by ensuring that you spend time with all groups over a period of time.

Providing for pupils with high ability

The needs of pupils with high ability should receive close attention. It is unacceptable to leave them to fend for themselves by claiming that they are adept at following written guidelines. While it is sometimes good for the ablest children to practise their independence as learners, they also need to be challenged, as the following contributions make clear.

REFLECTIVE TASK

Reflecting on alternative viewpoints

A cluster of rural schools arranged periodic study days for a group of high-ability learners drawn from each school. The focus of the study days was philosophy, and the children were presented with challenging activities in areas as diverse as formal logic, moral reasoning and semantics.

Consider the following key points taken from the feedback of the children and the head teachers of the participating schools.

»   *What lessons can you draw from their comments that can enhance your teaching of very able pupils?*

Children's feedback:

*   *It was great to work in a group. I often have to work on my own at my school.*

*   *The work was really hard, much harder than I usually have to do.*

*   *I learned that you can't always find out what a word means by looking in the dictionary. You have to think about the context in which it is used.*

*   *I enjoyed doing a subject that isn't part of the regular timetable.*

*   *I didn't feel patronised by the teacher, but I often do at school.*

Head teachers' feedback

*   *I've noticed that the child who attended the sessions has been using some of the techniques she learned at them back in her classroom.*

*   *The children were shocked to be confronted with things they couldn't do, and some of them simply gave up. I've learned that it's vital for the high-ability pupils to be really challenged at their own level regularly.*

*   *Because we've been concentrating on getting everyone to Level 4 in Year 6 we've lost sight of the importance of stretching all our children, especially those who will get well beyond Level 4 and those who are very unlikely to achieve it.*

> • *Tremendous opportunity for social contact with their intellectual peers. So often the very able child finds it hard to fit in socially, especially in a rural school where he or she is on a different academic plane from all the other children.*
>
> • *At our school we've decided to ask the philosophy tutor who led the children's study days to lead a session at our next Teacher Day. The emphasis will be on challenging the staff with something that we'll struggle to achieve. It's important to know what it feels like to find learning hard, and to be reminded that in many spheres of learning there are no clear answers.*

Among the precepts that govern the teaching of very able pupils are:

• offering a real challenge, at the individual's level;

• teaching a repertoire of thinking skills, to promote a critical, analytical disposition;

• valuing the use of the imagination by fostering divergent thinking;

• accepting the fact that your own knowledge may in some respects be outstripped by that of the pupils;

• encouraging resilience and determination when faced by difficulties.

As with the teaching of pupils with SEN, these points can be generalised, since they represent good teaching, whoever the pupils may be.

Summarising the characteristics of an inclusive classroom

The extent of diversity in your classroom is likely to be in proportion to the number of pupils in your class. All pupils are unique, yet you are doing your best both to address their individual circumstances and to weld them together as a class. This is a demanding task, and you will find it helpful to check periodically on the extent to which your practice is continuing to match your aspirations.

As Hyland aptly remarks, 'there is little point in simply promoting *equality* of opportunity within the school without promoting *quality* of opportunity' (Hyland, 2007, p 158). There are various ways of evaluating your work to check the extent to which *all* children are likely to find your classroom a welcoming place providing a positive experience. Here are some audit questions. More extensive checklists and prompts can be found in Macpherson (2007, pp 112f) and Glazzard (2011, pp 71–75).

One approach is to examine the room itself.

• Do the images and text displayed around the room reflect a range of aspects of social, cultural and linguistic diversity?

• Do the bookshelves contain a wide variety of texts, fiction and non-fiction, likely to appeal to boys and girls with different interests?

- Are there positive images of disability and are suitable adaptations in place for disabled pupils who may be in your class?

Another is to audit the curriculum.

- Does the range of people studied in history and RE reflect diversity in terms of gender, ethnicity and faith?

- Is a global dimension apparent in geography, and does it avoid stereotyping nations and groups?

- What range of texts do children encounter in literature, and are there examples with which each of your pupils can identify?

Thirdly, you should review how you present yourself to the children in your class.

- Do you pronounce and spell children's names correctly?

- Do you convey an implication that it is atypical not to live with two parents, a mother and father?

- Do you engage with *all* the children in personal talk about their interests, views and feelings?

Adapting your teaching to meet the needs of your pupils is not only about the formal curriculum. As the foregoing checklists suggest, it is children's encounter with the whole curriculum, and with those who teach it, that provides the true measure of your success.

Performance of understanding

Thinking about the school in which you work or have recently worked, respond to the prompts after each intended learning outcome, as a means of identifying your knowledge and understanding of the issues covered in the chapter.

- *your knowledge of how and when to use a variety of ways of differentiating teaching;*
  - Give an account of a time when you consciously planned an aspect of the formal curriculum to take advantage of knowledge brought by pupils from beyond the school.
  - Provide three examples of planned differentiation in your teaching, exhibiting (a) differentiation by outcome, (b) differentiation by task and (c) differentiation by support.

- *an awareness of factors that may inhibit pupils' ability to learn, and an enhanced capacity to overcome these;*
  - Identify two different pupils whose ability to learn was inhibited by factors outside of school, and explain how you enabled them to overcome these impediments.

- Articulate some examples to demonstrate that you are aware of the importance of the values that you portray to children, and that you monitor carefully the impressions that you may be giving them.

- *an understanding of pupils' physical, social and intellectual development, and an ability to adapt your teaching to cater for pupils' developmental needs as learners;*

  - Define what you understand by pupils' social development, and identify some ways in which you have adapted teaching and learning approaches with a view to enhancing children's social development.

  - Give examples showing how you have made use of assessment outcomes when designing differentiated tasks.

- *your appreciation of the needs of all pupils, especially those with special educational needs, those of high ability, those with English as an additional language and those with disabilities;*

  - Explain two or three occasions in your teaching when you have adapted your teaching in response to the identified needs of learners with SEN.

  - Identify and evaluate a short list of strategies to use in supporting pupils with EAL.

  - In what ways have you ensured that pupils with high ability have encountered challenge and had to extend themselves in their learning?

- *your ability to use and evaluate distinctive teaching approaches to engage and support all learners;*

  - Describe how you go about ensuring that all pupils feel welcomed and valued in your classroom.

  - Explain how you evaluate the teaching and learning approaches that you use. In what ways do you consider their differential benefits and drawbacks for various members of the class?

Taking it further

Evans, C and Waring, M (2008) Trainee Teachers' Cognitive Styles and Notions of Differentiation. *Education and Training*, 50 (2): 140–54.

Glazzard, J (2011) Including all Learners, in Hansen, A (ed) *Primary Professional Studies*. Exeter: Learning Matters.

Macpherson, P (2007) Creating a Positive Classroom Climate, in Jacques, K and Hyland, R (eds) *Professional Studies: Primary and Early Years*. Third edition. Exeter: Learning Matters.

References

Ainscow, M (2007) Taking an Inclusive Turn. *Journal of Research in Special Educational Needs*, 7 (1): 3–7. London: DCSF. Available online at www.nationalstrategies.standards.dcsf.gov.uk/personalisedlearning (accessed 27 January 2014).

Blatchford, P, Russell, A and Webster, R (2012) *Reassessing the Impact of Teaching Assistants*. Abingdon: Routledge.

Cortazzi, M and Lixian, J (2007) Speaking, Listening and Thinking: Metacognitive Approaches to Promoting Oracy. *Early Child Development and Care*, 177 (6–7): 645–60.

Department for Education and Employment (DfEE) (1994) *Code of Practice on the Identification and Assessment of Special Educational Needs*. London: DfEE.

Department of Education and Science (DES) (1985) *Education for All: Report of the Committee of Enquiry into the Education of Children from Ethnic Minorities*. (The Swann Report) Cmnd. 9453. London: DES.

Department for Education and Skills (DfES) (2001) *Code of Practice on the Identification and Assessment of Children with Special Educational Needs*. London: DfES.

Eaude, T (2012) *How Do Expert Primary Classteachers Really Work?* Northwich: Critical Publishing.

Ewens, T (2007) Spiritual, Moral, Social and Cultural Values in the Classroom, in Jacques, K and Hyland, R (eds) *Professional Studies: Primary and Early Years*. Third edition. Exeter: Learning Matters.

Frederickson, N and Cline, T (2009) *Special Educational Needs, Inclusion and Diversity*. Maidenhead: Open University Press.

Gardner, J (2006) Children who have English as an Additional Language, in Knowles, G (ed) (2006) *Supporting Inclusive Practice*. London: David Fulton.

Glazzard, J (2011) Including All Learners, in Hansen, A (ed) *Primary Professional Studies*. Exeter: Learning Matters.

Goepel, J, Childerhouse, H and Sharpe, S (2014) *Inclusive Primary Teaching: A Critical Approach to Equality and Special Educational Needs*. Northwich: Critical Publishing.

Gray, C and White, A L (2002) *My Social Stories Book*. London: Jessica Kingsley.

Hassan, N (2006) Race and Education, in Sharp, J, Ward, S and Hankin, L, *Education Studies: An Issues-Based Approach*. Exeter: Learning Matters.

Hyland, R (2007) Promoting Inclusion and Equal Opportunities, in Jacques, K and Hyland, R (eds) *Professional Studies: Primary and Early Years*. Third edition. Exeter: Learning Matters.

Lloyd, C (2008) Removing Barriers to Achievement: A Strategy for Inclusion or Exclusion? *International Journal of Inclusive Education*, 12 (2): 221–36.

Macpherson, P (2007) Creating a Positive Classroom Climate, in Jacques, K and Hyland, R (eds) *Professional Studies: Primary and Early Years*. Third edition. Exeter: Learning Matters.

Mistry, M and Sood, K (2012) Raising Standards for Pupils Who Have English as an Additional Language (EAL) through Monitoring and Evaluation of Provision in Primary Schools. *Education 3–13*, 40 (3): 281–93.

Mittler, P (2000) *Working Towards Inclusive Education: Social Contexts*. London: David Fulton.

Portwood, M (2007) *Developmental Dyspraxia: Identification and Intervention: A Manual for Parents and Professionals*. Abingdon: Routledge.

Safford, K and Drury, R (2013) The 'Problem' of Bilingual Children in Educational Settings: Policy and Research in England. *Language and Education*, 27 (1): 70–81.

Smith, C (2006) From Special Needs to Inclusive Education, in Sharp, J, Ward, S and Hankin, L, *Education Studies: An Issues-Based Approach*. Exeter: Learning Matters.

6 Using assessment accurately and productively

Learning outcomes

By the end of this chapter you should have developed and clarified:

- *your knowledge and understanding of how to assess the various curriculum areas, including statutory assessment requirements;*

- *an ability to use formative and summative assessment to secure pupils' progress;*

- *confidence in recording outcomes accurately and economically, and in sharing these with appropriate professionals, parents and pupils;*

- *an understanding of how to use relevant data to monitor progress, set targets and plan subsequent lessons; and*

- *an ability to involve pupils in evaluating their own work by giving them regular feedback, both orally and through high-quality marking, and by encouraging them to respond to the feedback.*

Purposes of assessment

You will be involved in assessing pupils' performance and progress for much of your time in the classroom, whether or not you are conscious of doing so. This might include:

- reacting to puzzled expressions when you are trying to explain something;

- asking questions to check that children have understood a topic;

- responding to pupils' queries as the lesson progresses.

These are examples of assessment being undertaken during the course of your teaching. Reflecting on the information that you receive as part of assessment activities, such as the three points identified above, is a major component of your professional practice. Sometimes it takes place outside of the classroom, for example when you are marking children's work after a lesson, but more often it is an integral part of your work with the class. Constructive feedback during the lesson enhances learning while it is taking place (Harrison and Howard, 2009), whereas written feedback at a later date, while helpful, arrives when the lesson has 'gone cold'.

The purposes of assessment are many and varied, and include the following:

- measuring and recording pupils' attainment;

- diagnosing a pupil's difficulties;

- evaluating the success of your teaching;

- giving children oral and written feedback about their performance;

- reporting to parents/carers on their children's progress;

- tracking pupils' progress and achievement;

- producing records about progress and attainment to pass to a new school when a child moves;

- suggesting improvements that pupils can make;

- informing your subsequent planning;

- producing evidence on which to base targets for whole school improvement;

- checking the value of a teaching aid;

- drawing up an Individual Education Plan (IEP) for a pupil with special needs;

- monitoring the success of the lesson and changing course if necessary;

- administering statutory tests and tasks;

- profiling pupils' strengths and weaknesses;

- evaluating the curriculum;

- identifying what children need to tackle next;

- forming groups of pupils with similar levels of attainment;

- forming groups of pupils with mixed levels of attainment.

Experienced teachers have often routinised many of the procedures associated with these objectives, so that they appear to be operating on auto-pilot. Whether you are new to teaching or a seasoned practitioner, there is always considerable value in reflecting carefully on how and why you plan to assess pupils' progress during a lesson, a sequence of lessons or across a broader sweep of their learning.

REFLECTIVE TASK

Reflecting on your teaching

Look at the planning and record keeping for the core subjects relating to one week's teaching that you undertook recently, and reflect on the ways in which you made use of assessment.

» *Using the bulleted list of purposes of assessment, identify which of them featured in your work during the week concerned.*

» *To what extent had you actually planned to use assessment for those purposes?*

» *Are there any examples of approaches to assessment that you consider have become a routinised part of your regular practice?*

» *Are there any that you recognise only with hindsight as having occurred?*

Scrutinise particularly the parts of your documentation that refer to lesson evaluation. You may be in the habit of writing about this on a lesson-by-lesson basis, or as a daily or weekly overview. Identify any comments that you wrote that were related to procedure (for example, about how well you managed the class, dealt with transitions and so on), and others that were related to learning (for example, that reflect your endeavour to gauge the amount of progress made by the class, groups or individuals). At a very early stage of learning to teach, a teacher may write, 'This went well'. 'This went well' is likely to mean that the lesson was orderly, timekeeping was appropriate and transitions went smoothly. It says nothing about the extent of the children's learning.

» *On reflection, is there anything about your approach to evaluation that you need to review?*

Types of assessment

The lengthy list of purposes of assessment can be grouped under two main headings:

* *Summative* assessment, sometimes called assessment OF learning, refers to the formal measurement of outcomes at the end of a period of time. This includes national tests, assessments made for the purpose of reporting to parents, end-of-week spelling tests and end-of-year assessments to be reported to the next class teacher or the next school.

* *Formative* assessment, sometimes called assessment FOR learning, includes all the activities, many of them informal, undertaken to observe children's ongoing understanding, so that teaching can be tailored to their learning needs. For example, questioning children during the introduction to the lesson, and inviting them to ask questions, helps you to judge their understanding of the concepts that you are introducing, and the learning intentions and the tasks that you are setting.

There are other categories particularly relevant to educational assessment.

- *Evaluative* assessment relates to the activity identified in the reflective task above. Teachers' critical reflections on their own teaching, when focused on the process of learning, contribute to assessment by influencing decisions about subsequent lessons. Thus, evaluative assessment tends to be mainly formative in character.

- *Diagnostic* assessment is used to identify particular educational needs, for example when a teacher's review of an individual pupil's performance suggests that a more detailed consideration is needed. Specific tests and observations are used to pinpoint particular difficulties and to identify appropriate teaching strategies to help the pupil to progress. Diagnostic assessment is summative, insofar as it produces results to inform others (for instance, for use when drawing up an IEP), but also formative, in that it is designed to lead to more effective teaching and learning for the pupil concerned.

- *Ipsative* assessment relates to an approach in which an individual's summative performance is judged against his or her previous results, without reference to other members of the class.

Raiker (2007) locates these types of assessment on a continuum, illustrating the differing degrees of formality associated with each category, and demonstrating their interconnectedness. This is a helpful approach, since it discourages any temptation to classify assessment activities too tightly. For example, although a weekly spelling test is principally summative, it can also have a formative value. If the results are used to identify words that were most frequently misspelt, the teacher can include them in a subsequent test, and draw the pupils' attention to the correct way to spell them.

Arguably, Raiker does not go far enough in her exploration of the categories of assessment, as the following extracts from a staff room discussion suggest.

REFLECTIVE TASK

Reflecting on alternative viewpoints

Consider the points made in this conversation between members of staff in a primary school.

Teacher V: *I think we spend too long on assessing children at the end of a topic, and at the ends of years. By then it's too late to do anything with the results, and in any case they usually don't tell us anything we don't already know. Ongoing formative assessment is far better, because you can nip problems in the bud. That's far more helpful to the children.*

Teacher W: *I agree with you that assessment ought to be a continuous process, but parents want to know what their children have achieved during the year. So I think there's a place for summative tests. My issue with them is that you run the risk of teaching to the test, which narrows the curriculum and promotes memorisation rather than deep learning.*

Head teacher D: *It seems to me that we shouldn't be seeing summative and formative assessment as two different things. I think that all assessment can be formative, as long as you make productive use of the results. The difference is a matter of timescale. You're obviously right, V, that good teaching involves constantly reflecting on children's responses, so that you can intervene when necessary to correct misconceptions, revise a tricky point or get pupils back on track. Good marking and feedback is also crucial. I agree with you, W, that teaching to the test can impoverish real learning. However, I can think of several examples of summative test results helping us to improve our curriculum and our teaching. For instance, the breakdown of our KS2 maths tests a few years back showed that our children scored poorly in geometry compared with arithmetic. That made us review our teaching of shape and space, and over the years there has been a steady improvement in our outcomes in geometry. So I think that summative assessment can be a type of formative assessment. It takes longer to affect children's progress than ongoing classroom assessment, but ultimately its effects can be profound.*

Reflect on the points being made by the three contributors.

»   *If you were to be the next person to speak in the conversation, what points would you make?*

(By the way, notice how hard it is to follow the head teacher in any discussion – heads have a way of making their pronouncements sound like the last judgement.)

If you are persuaded to accept the views of the head teacher in this task, you might conclude that there is no point in categorising assessment as summative and formative. However, the prevailing terminology has currency, and helps to clarify the type of assessment being described. What is key is to concentrate on ensuring that you make the best use of all the information that you gain through assessment, so that it impacts positively on children's learning.

Using summative assessment

You may sometimes decide to employ a summative test, for example in order to check that spellings or tables have been learned, or to assess what pupils know, understand and can do at the end of a sequence of lessons. At certain points in children's primary school careers they will be required to take national tests or assessment tasks. Additionally, your school may routinely administer summative tests, or require teachers to undertake summative teacher assessments, to pinpoint the attainment of pupils at intervals during their time at the school.

Validity and reliability

For a summative assessment item to be worthwhile it needs to possess two characteristics which help to ensure that it is free from bias and distortion.

1.   *Validity* refers to the accuracy of an assessment–whether or not it measures what it is intended to measure. For example, a mathematics test designed to cover the

topics taught throughout the year would not be valid if all the questions were about number and none about shape. If your spelling test contained some words that had not been set to be learned, it would not be a valid test of that week's homework (although it could still be a valid test of spelling).

2. *Reliability* refers to the extent to which assessments are consistent. For example, a written test in which some pupils were given more time than others would be unreliable, as would a test in which different markers were more or less lenient. Or suppose you created two test papers to cover the same content, for example to provide for the eventuality that some pupils might be absent on the chosen test day by ensuring that an alternative set of questions would be available. The assessment would only be reliable if both sets of questions were equally difficult, so the reliability would be expressed as a correlation between scores on the two test papers.

You can be confident that national test questions have been carefully scrutinised to ensure their validity, and that they have been trialled to check for reliability. If you were to question the validity of national tests, it might be on the grounds that they do not cover the whole curriculum, and that they focus on that which is readily measurable while ignoring aspects of personal development which parents and wider society prize as key outcomes of a good education.

Assuming that your school chooses published assessment materials for any summative assessments that it decides to administer, you should again be assured about reliability and validity. Any concerns you may have should, therefore, relate only to summative tests that you decide to create yourself. It is important, then, to remember to consider how to make your test valid and reliable, as well as thinking about the knowledge, understanding and skills that you plan to assess.

In practice, consideration of validity and reliability tends to give rise to dilemmas. One that has a significant bearing on your work as a primary school teacher concerns the medium through which the assessment is carried out. Suppose you are assessing the mathematical knowledge, skills and understanding of your class by means of practical problems couched in story form. What judgements do you make about pupils recently arrived at the school for whom English is an additional language? Failure to answer the questions may be a function of their linguistic background, and may conceal an excellent grasp of mathematics if tested in their first language. Should you use a translator, so that you can find out about their mathematical knowledge by enabling them to work in their first language? Similarly, pupils known to have a specific learning difficulty in an area of language may not be able to demonstrate the extent of their mathematical understanding using your assessment tool. Does this undermine the reliability of your chosen test? There are no straightforward answers to these dilemmas. They do, however, challenge you to think carefully about the purpose of the assessment that you are conducting. Is it children's mathematics that you wish to test or is your prime intention to learn about children's mathematical knowledge as expressed in English? Designing an assessment that is both valid and reliable is not as easy as it may first seem.

Summative data and national reporting

National tests, designed and marked externally to the school, are an established feature of schools' and teachers' accountability. Aggregated results are published, except in the case of very small schools where publication would allow individual pupils to be identified, and the information is also used by Ofsted as evidence of the pupils' attainment when schools are inspected (Ofsted, 2013). Ofsted may decide to defer the inspection of a school at which high levels of attainment are sustained, and may bring forward an inspection in the event of an unexpected drop in attainment.

Data for each school are readily available, both to the staff of the school and to members of the public. For example, the online inspection report for a school contains an electronic link to the School Data Dashboard, showing the school's data compared with national test results, attendance statistics, the extent to which the school succeeded in closing the gap between disadvantaged and other pupils (intended as a check on the efficacy of the pupil premium policy) and contextual information about the school. Overall, the data provide an opportunity for benchmarking against national comparisons.

REFLECTIVE TASK

Reflecting on your reading

Visit the Ofsted website (www.ofsted.gov.uk/inspection-reports/find-inspection-report) and find recent reports for two different primary schools known to you. Make yourself familiar with the format of the reports in those sections where attainment is reported, and compare what is said about the educational outcomes of the two schools. Look at the data available on the School Data Dashboard.

»   *Reflect on the extent to which the inspectors' findings, and the data on the dashboard, tally with your impressions of the schools.*

»   *Where there are differences, what are they, and what might account for them?*

Consider how teachers might be able to make productive use of the reports as a stimulus for development. This might include reinforcing the strengths that are identified as well as addressing the points requiring attention or improvement.

»   *In particular, do the data on the dashboard convey any messages about potential areas for action?*

Sometimes, external assessments provide sobering feedback for the staff of a school. Most teachers are positive in the way in which they encourage and praise their pupils for their effort and progress, and it can be dispiriting if the end results of their labours are reported as being below the national average. Yet an objective measure of pupils' attainment can be an important corrective to over-optimistic subjective judgements. After all, no teacher is in a position to compare the attainment of their current class with the national average performance of children of the same age. The hard data are the only available measures. While it would be wrong to downplay the significance of national test results, you should remember the importance of viewing them in the wider context of a school's inspection report. As well as academic achievement, inspectors also report on broader aspects of achievement, such as the spiritual, moral, social and cultural development of the pupils, their behaviour and the amount of progress that they make (Ofsted, 2013, p 17).

Attainment and achievement

A fundamental issue in the reporting of national test results concerns the difference between attainment and achievement.

* Attainment is measured against fixed standards. For example, the percentage of pupils at a school who reached the expected standard in national tests has been the subject of scrutiny, with a 'floor target' that all schools should meet being set by the Department for Education.

* Achievement, on the other hand, refers to the amount of progress made by pupils over a period of time. This requires a measure to be taken at the beginning and end of that period, for example a key stage, so that the progress made by each child can be determined. Aggregated data for a school give a 'value added' index.

You will appreciate that a school where many pupils started at a low level of attainment but made good progress will have a better value-added score than a school where pupils started at a high level and made only moderate progress, regardless of the fact that the first school might not have met the floor target whereas the second school did so. Both might claim to be the better school, one because it had the higher results, the other because its children made the greater amount of progress.

Public policy has been equivocal in this debate. While continuing to publish results of attainment, the coalition government has shown an increasing interest in value-added data relating to achievement. Paton (2013a) reports on action to challenge 'coasting schools', while Watt (2013) highlights an initiative designed to measure the effect of the 'pupil premium', a policy designed to target additional resources to the education of the most disadvantaged pupils. Research has shown that it is during the earliest years of primary education that children from disadvantaged backgrounds are most likely to fall behind their peers. For this reason, and because value-added assessment requires a baseline from which to gauge progress, Watt explains that ministers are keen to establish a means of assessing the knowledge and competence of pupils entering Year 1. The debate, which is ongoing, revolves around the extent to which the existing Early Years Foundation Stage (EYFS) profile (DfE, 2013) already provides suitable data. Ministers claim that measuring aggregated pupil progress from the Year 1 baseline to the Year 6 national tests will demonstrate the effectiveness of each school. This is hard to substantiate because of the numbers of children who move from school to school during their primary education. In a straw poll of a dozen head teachers, two reported that fewer than 50 per cent of their current Year 6 pupils had attended Year 1 in their school. Nevertheless, individual pupils' progress in the primary phase will understandably be of great interest to their parents.

Summative data and school improvement

Various sources of data are available to schools to enable them to track pupils' progress, especially in the core curriculum subjects, and to set realistic but challenging targets. The Fischer Family Trust (FFT), a non-profit company which processes the National Pupil Database for the DfE, provides data and analyses that teachers can use to set ambitious targets for pupils (www.fft.org.uk). RAISEonline (www.raiseonline.org) is a comprehensive data management facility. In addition to supporting schools with reports and analysis covering the attainment and progress of children in Key Stages 1 and 2, it incorporates interactive features allowing exploration of hypotheses about pupil performance.

By using these or similar tools schools can establish systems for tracking pupils' progress against targets. The use of profiling, for example looking at pupils' achievement across different aspects of a subject, can assist in identifying both major strengths and areas requiring attention.

You are likely to become involved in work linked to national summative data as part of whole school improvement activities. Schools' improvement plans are ideally devised as a result of discussion among the staff, with leadership from senior managers and subject leaders. Responding to the data for your school will probably be a major agenda item at staff meetings, and will form the basis of some staff-development activities.

REFLECTIVE TASK

Reflecting on your teaching

With respect to the school in which you teach, or have recently taught, look at the current version of the school improvement plan, and read it alongside the most recent data available, for example through FFT, RAISEonline or the School Data Dashboard. Reflect on the way in which your school's development is being shaped in response to the data about pupils' attainment and achievement.

» *To what extent do you find this a helpful way of maintaining a sense of realism about your school's performance?*

» *Does attention to the detail of the data, most of which are confined to core curriculum subjects, have the effect of narrowing the perspectives of members of staff?*

Future trends in national testing and data publication

Glaser (1963) described a distinction to be drawn between two types of test.

1. *Norm-referenced tests.* In these each candidate's performance is compared to that of everyone else who took the test. Thus, the mark achieved by the candidate at the 50th percentile is the mean average. Others are above or below average. Normative

assessment may be helpful in selective situations, for example if recruiters wish to identify the top 10 per cent of performers. However, this approach says nothing about the level achieved by the population being tested.

2.   *Criterion-referenced tests.* Here the criteria for achieving a certain standard of performance are set out in advance of the test. Theoretically, therefore, every candidate could pass, by reaching the set standard, and all might fail, if no-one reached the standard. For example, if the criterion is that candidates can correctly multiply together two single-digit numbers, the test would contain examples of that process. Assessors would agree on a pass mark (known as the 'cutscore') high enough to allow for careless errors while testing for the criterion under consideration.

Formerly, when a selection test (the 11 plus exam) was in place throughout England, normative testing was used to allocate a certain percentage of pupils to grammar schools, and this still happens, for example, in Kent. Recent and current trends, based on a standards-led agenda, fit well with a criterion-referenced assessment regime. Thus, the level of a pupil's performance is determined by means of teacher assessments through which teachers 'level' children's work, and by using formal tests. In both cases the level is judged with reference to published criteria. A public consultation on future arrangements for assessment and reporting of pupils' attainment (Paton, 2013b) reflects ministers' interest in re-introducing a degree of normative assessment. The proposal is predicated on the arguments that:

*   parents are interested in knowing how their children are performing in comparison with their peers nationally; and

*   schools (particularly at primary/secondary transfer) need reliable data when setting pupils by ability in the core curriculum subjects.

Parents and schools would be informed of the performance band (bands 1 to 10) within which children are placed in each subject following the Key Stage 2 national tests. Paton reports on a range of responses to the proposals. Whatever the outcome of the debate, the question of whether a school's performance is better measured by raw scores or value-added measures will remain unresolved.

Using formative assessment

Literature about formative assessment usually refers to a continuous process of interaction between teacher and learner whereby the learner's progress is constantly reviewed in the interests of enhancing effective learning. It is often described as 'assessment for learning'. However, Briggs helpfully draws a distinction between 'assessment for learning' and 'assessment as learning' (Briggs, 2011, p 185). She points out that, while teachers routinely notice and reflect on what children are doing during a lesson and intervene to correct, re-teach or extend their learning, they also help pupils to evaluate their own learning, for example by reviewing their work against success criteria. These two strands of formative assessment can be seen in the ten principles for learning devised by the Assessment Reform Group, in which assessment for learning is summarised as follows.

Assessment for learning should:

1. *be part of effective planning of teaching and learning;*

2. *focus on how students learn;*

3. *be recognised as central to classroom practice;*

4. *be regarded as a key professional skill for teachers;*

5. *be sensitive and constructive because any assessment has an emotional impact;*

6. *take account of the importance of learner motivation;*

7. *promote commitment to learning goals and a shared understanding of the criteria by which they are assessed;*

8. *give learners constructive guidance about how to improve;*

9. *develop the learners' capacity for self-assessment so that they can become reflective and self-managing;*

10. *recognise the full range of achievement of all learners.*

(Assessment Reform Group, 2002)

Observing and responding

The skill of observation is crucial to your ability to give children constructive feedback on their work. In the early stages of learning to teach it is natural for your observations to be concentrated on procedural matters, for example so that you can manage beginnings, transitions and conclusions of lessons. It is vital to build on this by extending your skills in observation to the sphere of learning. This is a key element enabling you to progress through the stages of professional development identified by Twiselton (2006), discussed in Chapter 4. Experienced teachers appear to be equipped with some sort of radar, since they seem able to react spontaneously to what is happening in the classroom. Sometimes they move to work quietly with an individual who has encountered a difficulty. At other times they bring together a group of children or even the whole class to work on an issue common to all of them. This apparently innate ability is the product of carefully honed skills systematically built up over time. The foundations of this process lie in first undertaking deliberately planned, focused observations, then gradually extending the scope of your practice until observing children's ongoing learning is an integral part of your repertoire of professional activities.

REFLECTIVE TASK

Reflecting on alternative viewpoints

Consider the comments of a relatively inexperienced mentor of trainee teachers, who was discussing her work with a university tutor.

Mentor L: *Yesterday I met our trainee teacher to discuss an English lesson that I had observed. Naturally, I wanted to get her talking about her impressions of the lesson, so I said, 'what did you notice during the main task?' She reeled off a list of things that she had noticed, but they were all about procedural matters: children who'd lost pencils, who needed the toilet, who called out, who all wanted her attention at the same time, who were being collected for a medical appointment, and so on. So I told her what I'd noticed: two children who'd become fascinated by rhyming words and discussed loads of examples that they would use in their poems, the fact that one child is still frequently reversing b and d, and that several are using bizarre pencil grips, the rich vocabulary evident in several children's work and the fact that some of them have transferred their learning about adverbs into their creative writing while others haven't. She was amazed. Of course, I had the benefit of being an observer rather than teaching the lesson, but I think I'd have seen most of those things if I'd been teaching it. I guess we have different preoccupations at different stages in our training.*

University Tutor M: *I'm sure that's right. What did you decide to do next?*

Mentor L: *We decided that I would teach the next lesson about poetry. We'll set out the intended learning outcomes, and the trainee will be an active observer. Her task will be to look for evidence that the children are addressing the ILOs, to identify examples where they are meeting them and to spot children who need further support. I've suggested she doesn't try to intervene in the lesson, but that she and I will compare notes afterwards, then jointly plan the following lesson so that we take action on what she has noticed. We'll also jointly mark the children's poems, using our school's marking policy. This expects us to give children credit for achieving the ILOs and suggest a next step, and also to explain to children any ways in which they have missed an ILO and what they need to do about it.*

University Tutor M: *It seems to me that you are working with your trainee in exactly the same way that you work with your class. If so, that's an excellent way of modelling the sort of practice you want her to develop. By helping her to focus her observation on a few, agreed criteria, you are building her capacity eventually to do that as an integral part of her teaching.*

» *As you reflect on this conversation, what can you take from it that can further enhance your own teaching?*

The need to engage in detailed observation in the course of your teaching, and to make it a customary part of your practice to give children prompt feedback and advice, is an example of routinisation, as described by Eraut (1994). As indicated in the mentor's comments, responding to children is sometimes immediate and sometimes a function of good practice in marking. Both can assist children's understanding of their own performance against known criteria.

Listening and questioning

Asking questions is obviously central to assessment. However, research (Raiker, 2007) has shown that the majority of questions asked by teachers are closed questions, requiring a short answer. While this can be a good way to check pupils' recall of straightforward facts, an open-ended style of questioning can help children to think more deeply, to respond more fully and to demonstrate their use of the discourse of the subject being studied. Raiker offers as an example the question, 'is 7 a prime number?' to which the only possible answers are 'yes', 'no', or 'I don't know'. In contrast, the question, 'Why is 7 a prime number?' requires a fuller response, involving knowledge of what a prime number is, use of subject-specific language and an explanation of reasoning (Raiker, 2007, p 53). This type of exchange illustrates the value and importance of dialogic teaching, reflecting Alexander's claim, 'Reading, writing and number may be the acknowledged curriculum "basics" but talk is arguably the true foundation of learning' (Alexander, 2004, p 5).

Engaging pupils in dialogue means that you need to listen attentively to what they say, not least because you will almost certainly need to ask follow-up questions to prompt them to extend their thinking still further. When you use open-ended questions, it is important to give children enough time to think about what you have asked and then frame a response. Whereas quick-fire, closed questioning may sometimes have its place in eliciting instant responses about matters of fact, thinking time is needed for a considered reply to a broader question. Raiker suggests that five seconds is an appropriate length of time for children to construct answers to open questions, whereas many teachers allow as little as one second before choosing a child to answer (Raiker, 2007, p 53). In classrooms where teachers allow more time to answer, children's involvement increases significantly, and more pupils participate. Harrison and Howard's examples of 'fat questions' demonstrate ways in which you can frame questions so as to promote thinking and discussion (Harrison and Howard, 2009, p 9).

The Assessment Reform Group analysed the shift in teachers' practices required to ensure that formative questioning can achieve its maximum benefit. They note that teacher/pupil discussions can often be characterised as a series of one-to-one discussions, with the teacher and one pupil involved in each set of exchanges, while the rest of the class looks on. They contrast this scenario with a more fruitful approach in which the teacher seeks to promote debate among class members, with the teacher as one participant among several. Harrison and Howard offer two contrasting methods for securing wider participation in class discussion, one involving posing the same question to two or more children consecutively, the other by setting up groups to consider a question and then report back at a plenary. They comment that 'This pushes the talk in the direction of the learners, which in itself is beneficial to learning, but also gives the teacher information about the current state of learning' (Harrison and Howard, 2009, p 15).

REFLECTIVE TASK

Reflecting on your reading

Harrison, C and Howard, S (2009) *Inside the Primary Black Box*. London: Nfer/Nelson.

In this short booklet, the authors summarise the implications for teaching in the primary and early years phases derived from research by the Assessment Reform Group based at King's College London. Read the section about questions and questioning on pages 9 to 16. Reflect on the ways in which your own practice might be enhanced through the adoption of some of their research-based suggestions.

Sharing objectives and discussing outcomes

You will be accustomed to deciding what you want the children to know by the end of a lesson or a sequence of lessons. In addition you will have gained some experience in differentiating learning intentions, so that they match the different levels of understanding of individuals and groups in the class. When drawing up your plans you make use of assessment outcomes, since a primary consideration is what the pupils already know and understand. Your information about this may come from summative tests, from formal and informal observations that you made during previous lessons and from your marking of children's work. Considering these data in the light of the area of the curriculum that the class is studying enables you to pinpoint the steps that you judge the children need to take next. Thus you frame new learning intentions or objectives. Whereas educational goals and aims are respectively medium- and long-term aspirations, learning intentions or objectives are short term in character. Draft them so that you express what you intend the class, or the group, or the individual to know, understand or be able to do by the end of the lesson. Examples would include, 'To be able to add two single-digit numbers accurately' or, 'To explain what a reversible process is'.

Sharing the learning intention with the pupils tells them the purpose of the lesson. When you discuss it with them, you will also need to include an explanation of the success criteria, in other words what they need to do to demonstrate their achievement of the objective. Learning intentions should be SMART (Specific, Measurable, Achievable, Realistic and Timebound) so that they can be assessed during the lesson. Raiker reviews the use of WALT (We are learning to …) to express learning intentions and WILF (What I am looking for…) to express success criteria as common vehicles for involving children in monitoring their own learning (Raiker, 2007, p 52). This can be a helpful way of working, as long as the children and all staff members are trained to appreciate the difference between completing an activity and demonstrating learning.

REFLECTIVE TASK

Reflecting on your teaching

Review a few of the lessons that you have taught recently.

» *In what ways have you ensured that the children understood what you intended them to learn in those lessons?*

» *How were they made aware of what would count as a demonstration of that learning?*

Investigate the discourse around learning intentions and success criteria used throughout your school.

» *To what extent is there a common approach that children would perceive as a systematic way of working? What might you do to enhance your own practice?*

A good way of helping children to develop their understanding of how to use the cycle of learning intentions and success criteria to improve their work is to involve them in peer assessment and self-assessment. For example, you might give them an anonymised piece of work and ask them to work in pairs to identify whether it meets the declared learning intention in the light of the published success criteria. Children quickly become adept at undertaking this task, and can be asked to suggest ways in which the work could be improved. This familiarises them with a range of strategies that can be used by learners as self-help activities, from re-reading to re-calculating and asking a question to prompt re-thinking. You could next ask your pupils to engage in the same process with a piece of their own work, evaluating and improving it before submitting it to be marked. Children particularly enjoy using sticky notes to give themselves reminders that suggest how their own or others' work could be improved.

Marking and written feedback

Marking children's work helps you to gain an understanding of the progress made by all the pupils in the class, not just those with whom you worked during a particular lesson. Carefully marked work, with comments linked to learning intentions and success criteria, forms part of your record keeping, which is a good reason for asking children to date their work. The interests of formative assessment are obviously best served if you can mark work while it is in progress, since your feedback can be put to immediate use. However, there is also an important place for the considered judgements that you make when you are able to focus on pieces of work away from the classroom.

Briggs draws attention to the work of Val Brooks (Briggs, 2011, p 189), whose research shows that even teachers with a firm grasp of criterion-based assessment continue to make subjective judgements when marking children's work, for example by using the criteria to confirm decisions they have already made, or by seeking to make positive points in the face of negative evidence. Your marking needs to be both honest and related to the intended learning. Resist any temptation to give credit for achievement in the absence of achievement. Written feedback can still be sensitive and can credit effort, but you must tell the truth, albeit in a constructive way. After all, if a child has missed the success criteria, it is your responsibility to find an alternative way forward, and your feedback can indicate this.

Good written feedback will explain to the child and other readers (parents, colleagues and inspectors, for example) the positive features of the work and will offer suggestions and prompts by way of 'scaffolding' to enable the pupil to make improvements. This is time-consuming but its value is confirmed by the consequences of doing it well. Butler's (1987) research suggests that feedback is most effective when teachers do not try to grade an item as well as writing a formative comment. If a mark, level or grade is given, this becomes the focus of attention for the pupils, and they overlook the comment. When teachers concentrate on the written comment, their feedback tends to become more detailed as well as being personalised. Written feedback to individuals can usefully be accompanied by oral feedback to groups or the whole class, since this allows you to deal with issues common to several pupils in an economic way.

Since a major purpose of written feedback is that it should feed forward into subsequent learning, it is important to allocate time for children to work with their feedback. This can helpfully include asking them to produce a response to your comments to indicate to you how they have gone about the task of improving their own work and engaging in self-evaluation.

REFLECTIVE TASK

Reflecting on your teaching

Examine a number of pieces of work that you have marked formatively over a period of time. Evaluate the written feedback that you have given to the children, reflecting on whether it made reference to the learning intentions and success criteria, and the extent to which it made clear suggestions to the children about how to improve their work.

Profiling

The use of profiling can be a profitable way of addressing the assessment of individuals, groups and a whole class. A record showing a child's attainment across a range of subjects can obviously identify strengths and weaknesses in the various areas of the curriculum. You can investigate the pupil's performance more closely by profiling attainment in different aspects of a subject, for example arithmetic computation, understanding of ratio and percentages, and knowledge of shape and space in mathematics. This sort of information can be used summatively, as a ready means of recording the child's attainment, and formatively, as the basis for targeting future teaching and learning. Sharply focused profiling instruments, often used by educational psychologists, can offer detailed diagnostic assessments to identify specific difficulties in learning and suggest appropriate interventions.

By aggregating children's profiles you can display the outcomes of groups and the whole class. This provides you with evidence when evaluating your teaching. For example, if a majority of your class consistently performs less strongly in one subject, or a particular aspect of a subject, you quickly realise that this area calls for prompt attention. You can also use aggregated profiles to study the differential performance of groups within the class, for example boys and girls.

Recording and reporting

Record keeping is an activity that can easily develop a life of its own, so that it takes up a vastly disproportionate amount of your time. It is, however, both important and necessary, as the following list of purposes of recording indicates:

- to show what children have covered;

- to indicate progress made;

- to show results of summative assessments;

- to inform subsequent planning based on individual pupils' learning;

- to provide evidence of what children know, understand and can do;

- to inform reviews of IEPs;

- to form a basis on which to set future targets;

- to give information for inclusion in reports to parents;

- to facilitate discussion at parents' evenings;

- to help when preparing reports for the next teacher or school.

Contemporaneous records are invaluable in providing a trail enabling you to track a pupil's progress, rather than relying on recollections, which may be fallible.

Most schools operate an agreed system of record keeping, which you will be required to adhere to, and this will probably include maintaining a portfolio or e-portfolio for each pupil. You will also find it helpful to supplement the school's requirements with more informal recordings of your own. Remember that parents have a right to see any records kept about their child, so ensure that what you write is fair and objective. Among the strategies that you can use to record formative observations economically are:

- annotating your lesson plans;

- using sticky labels;

- creating grids and even spreadsheets;

- taking photographs (check your school's policy).

Briggs (2011, pp 56–58) explores the value of each of these. You should be aware of the importance of dating records. Tracking pupils' progress is rendered impossible if you cannot put your written records into date order.

Your school has a statutory duty to send at least one written report to parents each year, and to publish its arrangements for discussing it with parents and carers. In practice, many schools exceed this minimum. Additionally, parents will sometimes wish to discuss their child's progress at other times during the year, underlining the importance of keeping records up to date.

Schools have considerable flexibility over the style and content of their report forms, as long as the following are included at least annually:

- a summary of the child's achievement during the year in each area of the curriculum;

- information about strengths and areas for development;

- details of attendance;

- results of any statutory assessment;

- details of any IEP, especially if revisions have occurred;

- information about parents' opportunity to discuss the report with school staff.

As with the records that you keep, reports must be in sufficient detail to convey information about progress, attainment and achievement. While it is appropriate to make comments about effort and attitude, that must never become a substitute for hard evidence about what a child knows, understands and can do.

REFLECTIVE TASK

Reflecting on your schooldays

» *What do you recall about reports that were written about you when you were at primary school? Have you perhaps seen reports written about older generations of your family?*

» *How informative were they?*

» *What did they tell you about curriculum coverage or what the individual had achieved?*

The author's reports, from the 1950s and 1960s, had a mark out of ten for each subject (out of 20 for English and arithmetic), followed by a very brief comment. The number of absences was recorded, followed by 'position in class' and a brief summative sentence from the class teacher and two or three words from the head teacher. If you have seen reports like that, your comment on their format and content may well be, 'Not good enough', or 'Must try harder'.

Performance of understanding

Thinking about the school in which you work or have recently worked, respond to the prompts after each intended learning outcome, as a means of identifying your knowledge and understanding of the issues covered in the chapter.

* *your knowledge and understanding of how to assess the various curriculum areas, including statutory assessment requirements;*

    - Describe how, in your approach to assessing pupils' progress in mathematics, you include a profile of their achievement across the different components of the subject.

    - Explain the rationale behind the Year 1 phonics screening check and how you would administer it.

* *an ability to use formative and summative assessment to secure pupils' progress;*

    - Give examples of how you have made use of formative assessment during lesson introductions and main tasks to enhance children's learning.

    - In what ways have you made use of the outcomes of summative assessments to review the curriculum and/or your approaches to teaching and learning in order to improve pupils' attainment?

- *confidence in recording outcomes accurately and economically, and in sharing these with appropriate professionals, parents and pupils;*

  - Explain the ways in which you make informal records based on your ongoing formative assessment during lessons. What do you do with these records so that they have a positive impact on subsequent learning?

  - Identify two or three examples of how you have reported to parents on their child's progress, either in writing or orally. How can you ensure that there is a shared understanding between you and the parents about the report that you have given?

- *an understanding of how to use relevant data to monitor progress, set targets and plan subsequent lessons;*

  - Explain how a teacher in Year 1 could make productive use of the information contained in pupils' EYFS profiles.

  - Describe how teachers in Key Stage 2 can use RAISEonline data and the School Data Dashboard when planning, setting targets and monitoring pupils' progress.

- *an ability to involve pupils in evaluating their own work by giving them regular feedback, both orally and through high-quality marking, and by encouraging them to respond to the feedback.*

  - Identify two or three examples from your teaching of occasions when you intervened with questions or other oral feedback which led pupils to evaluate their work and find ways of improving it.

  - Explain how you use marking to help children to understand the strengths and weaknesses of their work in a constructive and sensitive way. In what ways have pupils responded to your written feedback?

Taking it further

Briggs, M, Woodfield, A, Martin, C and Swatton, P (2008) *Assessment for Learning and Teaching in Primary Schools*. Second edition. Exeter: Learning Matters.

Harrison, C and Howard, S (2009) *Inside the Primary Black Box*. London: Nfer/Nelson. RAISEonline. Available online at www.raiseonline.org (accessed 26 February 2014).

References

Alexander, R (2004) *Towards Dialogic Teaching: Rethinking Classroom Talk*. Cambridge: Dialogos.

Assessment Reform Group (2002) *Assessment for Learning: 10 Principles. Research-Based Principles to Guide Classroom Practice*. Available online at www.assessmentreformgroup.files.wordpress. com/2012/01/10principles_english.pdf (accessed 27 February 2014).

Briggs, M (2011) Assessment, in Hansen, A (ed) *Primary Professional Studies*. Exeter: Learning Matters.

Butler, R (1987) Task-Involving and Ego-Involving Properties of Evaluation: Effects of Differential Feedback Conditions on Motivational Perceptions, Interest and Performance. *Journal of Educational Psychlogy*, 79 (4): 474–82.

Department for Education (DfE) (2013) *Early Years Foundation Stage Profile: Handbook 2014*. STA/14/7088. London: DfE. Available online at www.gov.uk/government/publications/early-years-foundation-stage-profile-handbook-2014 (accessed 26 February 2014).

Eraut, M (1994) *Developing Professional Knowledge and Competence*. London: Routledge Falmer.

Glaser, R (1963) Instructional Technology and the Measurement of Learning Outcomes. *American Psychologist*, 18: 510–22.

Harrison, C and Howard, S (2009) *Inside the Primary Black Box*. London: Nfer/Nelson.

Ofsted (2013) The Framework for School Inspection. Available online at www.ofsted.gov.uk/resources/framework-for-school-inspection (accessed 25 February 2014).

Paton, G (2013a) League Tables Overhauled in 'Coasting Schools' Crackdown. *The Daily Telegraph*, 14 October 2013.

Paton, G (2013b) Primary School Children to be Ranked in Exam Overhaul. *The Daily Telegraph,* 17 July 2013.

Raiker, A (2007) Assessment for Learning, in Jacques, K and Hyland, R (eds) *Professional Studies: Primary and Early Years*. Third edition. Exeter: Learning Matters.

Twiselton, S (2006) The Problem with English: The Exploration and Development of Student Teachers' English Subject Knowledge in Primary Classrooms. *Literacy*, 40 (2): 88–96.

Watt, N (2013) Five-Year-Olds Could Face National Tests. *The Guardian*, 17 July 2013.

7 Managing pupils' behaviour

Learning outcomes

By the end of this chapter you should have developed and clarified:

* *an understanding of the importance of rules and routines for behaviour in classrooms;*

* *confidence in your ability to promote good behaviour in the classroom and around the school;*

* *your knowledge of a range of strategies for managing pupils' behaviour, and an ability to use them consistently and effectively;*

* *an understanding of ways of matching your behaviour management strategies to children's developmental needs; and*

* *an ability to form and maintain an appropriate teacher/pupil relationship with individuals, groups and classes.*

Good behaviour as an educational aim

A group of newly appointed primary school governors attended an induction event, at which they tried to define the qualities they would look for if interviewing for a new teacher at their school. When asked to recall their own schooldays, and to identify the key attributes of good teachers who had taught them, each individual mentioned an aspect of discipline or behaviour management. The course tutor struggled in vain to get them to identify anything about the teachers' subject knowledge or skills in explaining, questioning or marking. The emphasis for each governor was on the importance of a firm but fair approach to managing a class. Hay/McBer's (2000) research with school pupils, reviewed in Chapter 1, elicited similar responses. Children look to teachers to operate a firm but fair classroom régime so that teaching and learning can proceed unhindered by misbehaviour or disruption.

REFLECTIVE TASK

Reflecting on your schooldays

Think about your own schooldays, if possible during the primary years, and identify what you most readily recall about some of the teachers who taught you.

» *Are your recollections similar to those of the school governors mentioned in the preceding paragraph, who focused on teachers' approaches to discipline?*

» *What opinions and beliefs about behaviour, some of them perhaps unexamined, do you bring with you into your own practice as a teacher?*

An emphasis in recent years on the importance of achieving the highest possible educational outcomes might misleadingly give an impression that behaviour management has been reduced in importance. Nothing could be further from the truth, since an orderly classroom is a prerequisite of effective teaching and learning. However, classroom discipline is a more complex topic than is sometimes assumed. You need both clarity of aims and a broad repertoire of approaches in order to ensure that your classroom is both orderly in terms of conduct and productive in terms of educational attainment.

Teachers' responsibility for pupils' moral development

The 1944 Education Act viewed the purpose of education as 'the spiritual, moral, mental and physical development of the community' (DES, 1944, section 7). Responsibility for cultural development was added in the Education Reform Act of 1988 (DES, 1988), and social development was added in 1992, when Ofsted was established (DfE, 1992). Ofsted's decision to inspect spiritual, moral, social and cultural development (SMSC) in a discrete part of its reports on schools had the unfortunate effect of separating these four categories from those of mental and physical development (Ewens, 2007). This gave the impression that teaching and learning of the formal curriculum could be separated from the broader task of nurturing children and young people, with the promotion of good standards of behaviour placed in the latter category. In reality the two endeavours are logically and practically intertwined.

Society's expectation that schools will promote good conduct is both an aim in itself and a means to an end. As an overarching aim, it fosters an aspiration that a school should be a safe place where pupils, whatever their background, learn to live harmoniously with others, respecting both other children and adults. This approach, which sees the school as a microcosm of wider society, expects teachers to encourage pupils to be appreciative of, and sensitive to, their own and other people's beliefs and opinions, cultural values and practices, and to promote high standards of behaviour in terms of personal integrity, interpersonal relationships and respect for property and the environment. The ultimate aim is that pupils will achieve the self-discipline necessary to succeed in 'the opportunities, experiences and responsibilities of adult life' (DES, 1988). Parents frequently comment during parents' evenings on whether their child is happy at school. This reflects a concern on their part to be reassured that their child is socially well adjusted, and able to interact comfortably and appropriately with peers and adults alike. A school's reputation for high standards of behaviour and warm mutual relationships appears to play a greater role in parents' judgements than information about raw assessment outcomes.

A narrower, but equally important, approach sees behaviour management as a means to an end. In this view, teachers are expected to inculcate positive standards of behaviour so that teaching and learning can be pursued without disruption. This is the central thrust of Adams' (2009, 2011) and Ellis and Tod's (2009) writing and is reflected in their titles, all of which refer to 'behaviour for learning'. Apart from the obvious need to gain the attention of the class at the start of any lesson, you may be surprised by the complexity inherent in the concept of behaviour for learning. For example, you need to consider the different types of behaviour that are appropriate in a variety of curriculum areas. Children may need to be physically and vocally active in some activities involving teamwork, whereas you might want them to remain silent in tasks requiring an individual response, especially when sustained periods of concentration are called for. When planning and introducing a lesson you should therefore include instructions about the sorts of behaviour that you expect as well as outlining the tasks to be tackled and the learning outcomes that you envisage.

Working within the framework of a school's behaviour policy

Schools draw up behaviour policies to provide guidance for staff, so that the school's climate of relationships can be marked by consistency of purpose and procedure. You therefore need a good working knowledge of the aims and procedures outlined in the behaviour policy of the school in which you work.

REFLECTIVE TASK

Reflecting on your reading

Read the following extract from the behaviour policy of Primary School X, in which the key aims are set out.

Behaviour policy

The principal aims are:

* *to provide a happy and secure environment which enables individuals within the school community to develop their full potential;*

* *to enable the children to take their places as valued members of society;*

* *to encourage independence and respect for themselves, others and the world in which they live.*

Reflect on this list of aims in the light of the preceding paragraphs.

» *To what extent do you think School X has captured the essence of the education service's role in fostering good behaviour?*

> » *Do you have any suggestions for amendments or additions to these aims?*

Compare School X's list of aims with those found in the behaviour policy of the school in which you teach or have recently taught.

> » *Are there any key differences, and what are your thoughts on these?*

It is noteworthy from School X's aims that the school has both a long- and short-term vision for its pupils' development. Indeed, the very fact that a school has thought out the aims underpinning its approach to behaviour management may be a surprise to you.

When teachers begin their training, their first thought may be one of self-preservation, and of a need to assert command over the class from the outset. That is not an unworthy or inappropriate view, and it is not until you are confident in your ability to manage the class that you can begin to consider wider implications of behaviour management. The oft-quoted maxim, 'Don't smile until Christmas; don't laugh until Easter' contains the kernel of truth that it is easier to lighten your approach after a stern beginning than to tighten the discipline after a relaxed start.

REFLECTIVE TASK

Reflecting on alternative viewpoints

A chance meeting in the staff room between the Chair of Governors at School X, whose behaviour policy is quoted above, and Trainee teacher Q, who is nearing the end of a five-week placement at the school, led to an interesting conversation about managing pupils' behaviour.

Chair of Governors: *I hope you've found your time with us useful.*

Trainee teacher Q: *I have indeed. The biggest lesson that I've learned is about discipline. At first I concentrated on making sure I had control of the class, especially at the beginnings and ends of lessons, and at transition points. However, I've realised that the school is actually a working community which already has a set of values and straightforward rules that staff and pupils follow – at least most of the time. What I now appreciate is the importance of working within the existing systems, so that there is consistency for the children regardless of which of us – the class teacher or myself – is taking the lesson. On my next placement I shall make a point of finding out about the prevailing culture, both by reading the behaviour policy and also observing how the staff implement it, before I start to teach the class.*

Chair of Governors: *That's an interesting way of looking at it. But don't you also think that it's important for children to learn that adults differ in the detail of what they consider to be good behaviour? For example, there's one teacher in our school who always seems to have a very quiet classroom and another whose class usually produces a busy hum of activity. Both are good teachers and get pleasing results; they're just different people. So I don't think you need to feel that you ought necessarily to operate in exactly the same way as the class teacher, as long as you achieve a good standard of behaviour from your class.*

Trainee teacher Q: *I see your point. It's quite complicated, isn't it?*

Reflect on your own experience of managing a class in the light of this conversation.

»   *How much scope can teachers have to be different in their expectations of good
behaviour without the children being puzzled by apparent inconsistencies?*

Children's moral development

You need to be aware of how children learn in the sphere of morality, just as you need a
grasp of their development in language and number. Knowing how children's understanding of right and wrong typically develops is fundamental when deciding how best to manage
their behaviour. Central to a consideration of moral development is the work of Kohlberg
(1984). A constructivist, like Piaget (see Chapter 3), Kohlberg developed a stage theory of
the growth of moral understanding, which he built upon previous work undertaken by Piaget
himself. Reduced to its simplest components, Kohlberg's theory identifies three main phases
of moral development:

1.   *anomy*, literally 'absence of rules', characterised by the dominance of a pleasure/
pain principle. Very young infants' behaviour is dominated by the avoidance of
situations that give pain and adherence to what gives pleasure. Principles of right
and wrong do not yet feature;

2.   *heteronomy*, literally 'other people's rules', a stage at which children accept that
adults set out for them what is right and wrong, and determine the framework within
which their activities take place. The pleasure/pain principle morphs into a rewards/
sanctions regime, and the child accepts that it is part of the role of the nurturing
adult (parent, teacher, other figure of authority) to drive forward the moral code and
its associated consequences;

3.   *autonomy*, literally 'own rules', a stage at which moral judgements and codes are
becoming internalised, and the young person is becoming able to take responsibility
for moral decision making.

As with parallel examples of constructivist thinking, it is important not to treat these divi-
sions as fixed and clearly delineated. Indeed, Kohlberg himself later sub-divided them into
six phases (Murray, 2007). Progression from one stage to the next is necessarily gradual and
accompanied by periods of regression, but Kohlberg's approach helps to illuminate some
features of children's thinking and conduct in a way which is helpful to primary teachers.

REFLECTIVE TASK

Reflecting on your reading

McLeod, S.A. (2011) *Kohlberg – Moral Development – Simply Psychology*. Available online at
www.simplypsychology.org/kohlberg.html (accessed 15 November 2013).

McLeod offers a concise summary of Kohlberg's experiments and the conclusions that he drew from them. The article also presents a critique of his approach and its outcomes, notably in a review of Gilligan's (1977) response to Kohlberg which outlines objections to his methodology.

» *After reading McLeod's short article, summarise what you consider to be the central claims made by Kohlberg and the most significant questions raised by his critics.*

» *How might the debate sketched by McLeod help you to think about your role in helping children to develop moral thinking and behaviour?*

The key criticisms of Kohlberg's theory are as follows.

• He underplays the fact that there is more to moral behaviour than moral reasoning.

• There is a sex bias in his work, reflected in the samples chosen for his studies, which leads to an overemphasis on the concept of judgement and insufficient attention to qualities such as compassion.

These shortcomings do not, however, undermine Kohlberg's fundamental thesis, namely that children appear to pass through distinct phases in their moral thinking, and you can capitalise on his findings in your work with children about their behaviour.

For the most part, pupils at primary school will be operating at the level of heteronomy. They will expect adults to set the framework of conduct, monitor pupils' behaviour and use positive reinforcement to reward compliance and punish, or at least frown on, non-compliance. But, as Kohlberg himself recognised, his stage of heteronomy represents a broad continuum. At one end of the scale will be children who are just beginning to understand the notion that adults set the rules. These pupils will require regular exposure to explanations and reminders of the expected behaviours. At the other extreme will be children who are starting to test the boundaries, as they begin to become more independent in their moral thinking and behaviour. You must not suppose that it is necessarily the youngest children who are still at the earliest stage of learning, or the oldest who are ready to become more independent in their moral reasoning and conduct. The stages are not always congruent with ages, although there is understandably a trend for this to be the case.

From anomy to heteronomy

The early stages of formal education are characterised by the gradual introduction and development of a set of routines, by means of which young children become socialised. In situations as diverse as the ritual of washing hands before eating or encouragement to pay attention to a story being read, the early years practitioner is establishing the principle that procedures and practices are determined by adults and followed by children. While the pleasure/pain principle that drives Kohlberg's stage of anomy is still in evidence, not least in periods of time allocated to 'choosing' activities, the imposition of directed tasks is a marker of a shift towards heteronomy. This is important in terms of the formal curriculum, as it enables children to encounter aspects of the curriculum that they need to experience, but might otherwise choose to avoid. In terms of their relationships with peers and adults, the fact that the teacher sometimes directs children into particular groupings means that they meet and interact with others whom they might otherwise not choose to work with.

Notice how experienced primary teachers use the first person plural in their behaviour management discourse. 'We sit up straight like this', 'we take turns and share', 'we don't shout out': these and similar pronouncements are the stuff especially of infant classrooms. The first person plural, with its inclusive overtones, is a helpful device in the process of socialisation, making it clear to offenders that the teacher wants them to be part of a cohesive group, working to a common set of standards. If translated into the second person: 'you must sit up straight, take turns, not shout out', these strictures instantly become personalised and isolating, separating the deviant individual from the group. Consider the difference between saying, 'why aren't you ready, Paul?' and, 'We're waiting for you, Paul'. One is a personal criticism, the other an invitation to join the group. It is hard to resist drawing a parallel between the actions of a skilled teacher in bringing a class together with firm but kindly authority and the work of a well-trained sheepdog in rounding up a pack of lively ewes!

Another linguistic device aiding the establishment of the teacher's authority is associated with giving orders. Suppose you want to ask Shabana to close the door. An experienced teacher automatically gives the order first, then adds the 'magic word', followed by the child's name: 'Close the door, please, Shabana'. This may appear a trifling point, but it conceals vital issues. Leaving the child's name until last in the sentence means that the whole class needs to attend to what you are saying, since you might be going to ask any of them. Putting the command first emphasises your authority. Including 'please' models the good manners that the school is seeking to promote. This point can be transferred for use in your questioning technique as part of an approach to behaviour for learning. Reflect on the difference between saying, 'Franz, what is five threes?' and 'what is five threes, Franz?' If you mention Franz's name first, every other child in the class can switch off, but leaving his name until last means that all the children must listen in case you're going to ask them.

Ensuring that all of your pupils have reached Kohlberg's stage of heteronomy, and left behind the anarchic implications of anomy, is crucial to the establishment of good order in your classroom. Close attention to your use of language can make a considerable difference to your success in gaining and maintaining that order.

Within the phase of heteronomy

Most Ofsted reports on primary schools contain positive judgements about pupils' behaviour. Teachers' expertise in behaviour management is one factor. Another is the fact that children at the stage of heteronomy are more likely to be compliant, since they typically accept adult authority as the norm. This does not mean that your work in behaviour management is likely to be unproblematic. A major reason is that children come from a variety of backgrounds and have diverse prior knowledge and understanding of matters of right and wrong. Bringing together a class of pupils, or indeed a whole school, under the umbrella of an agreed ethos of values and conduct is difficult. Its complexity can be compared to the challenges that you face in making suitable provision in English and mathematics for the wide range of abilities and aptitudes found in your class.

In establishing your authority as the teacher in your classroom, you will need to have regard to the school's behaviour policy, so that the ways in which you work exhibit consistency with your colleagues' approaches. This is especially important during the phase of heteronomy. While accepting that adults have the right to set the rules, children at this stage of their moral development become keenly aware of the concept of fairness and they tend to find inconsistency a prime example of unfairness.

Rogers (1998) emphasises the importance of concise sets of rules and routines for behaviour, in classrooms and around the school, based on fairness. Periodic conversations about what makes a rule fair helps to embed the concept of fairness in pupils' understanding, and you can engage your class in discussions about amending rules, subject to your having the final veto. Pupils should regularly be made aware of the fair rules by visual and oral reminders, and your responses to children's conduct, whether good or bad, should include references to them. This way of working makes it clear to pupils that your feedback on their behaviour is based on publicly available criteria, rather than on your random personal whims, and helps you to avoid personal confrontation between teacher and pupil. The value of this approach will be strengthened in your classroom if you overtly model the conduct that you expect from the class, demonstrating that the fair rules govern your behaviour as well as that of the children.

Rogers' work, liberally illustrated with astute analyses of actual classroom incidents, also points to the value of positive strategies for managing behaviour. This notion is closely linked to the sequence of stimulus, response and reward associated with operant conditioning, derived from the work of Skinner and other behavioural psychologists (Benjamin, 2007). The underpinning idea is that positive reinforcement strategies prove more effective than the use of negative consequences in securing long-term changes in conduct. In order to explore this idea and its practical implications, consider a further extract from the behaviour policy of Primary School X and part of an interview with its head teacher.

REFLECTIVE TASKS

Reflecting on your reading

Extract from School X's behaviour policy

We believe that teachers have a right to teach and that children have a right to learn in an environment free from disruptive behaviour. This will be achieved through positive behaviour strategies.

We offer the children:

- *simple rules that set firm and fair limits for behaviour;*

- *a straightforward set of consequences and sanctions for both good and bad behaviour;*

- an opportunity to learn to manage their own behaviour;

- constant, positive encouragement;

- an opportunity to raise their self-esteem.

» Identify the key characteristics of behaviour management advocated by the head teacher and governors of School X in their behaviour policy.

» To what extent can the five bulleted points be viewed as responding to the three main stages of moral development identified by Kohlberg?

» In what ways do they draw upon the work of Rogers, described in the preceding paragraphs?

Reflecting on alternative viewpoints

Head teacher of School X: *Each year we hold a joint meeting between the staff and the governors. Last year the main focus was on behaviour. We concluded that our school should expect children to learn how to behave appropriately, just as they are expected to use language and number appropriately. When they join the school we want children to become accustomed to working and playing within a framework of simple rules and routines. By the time they leave us, we'd like them to be well on the way to managing their own conduct independently, just as we want them to be increasingly independent in their learning of the various school subjects. Of course we don't succeed all the time, whether in maths or behaviour, so we have a well-publicised system of sanctions, as well as a set of rewards. I'm particularly keen to ensure that no child is – or feels – ultimately excluded. There's so much evidence to show that pupils who experience exclusion – especially the ultimate sanction of being permanently excluded from a school – are far more likely than others to end up in trouble with the police. To avoid a trend towards exclusion, punishments are always linked with opportunities for forgiveness, reconciliation and restoration. Again, I'd emphasise the parallel with maths, or any other subject. Poor work in maths results in doing corrections and extra work, with the aim of improving achievement. The sanctions that result from poor behaviour are also designed to improve achievement. Our staff/governors meeting also made it clear that punishments should not be the consequence of teachers' anger, but that children should understand them as inevitable consequences of breaking the fair rules and routines that are the basis of school life. And for those who find it especially difficult to improve their behaviour, we respond as we would for those who find maths particularly hard, by providing extra support, one-to-one if necessary, rather than by imposing harsher penalties. It goes without saying that we discuss progress in behaviour with parents, and look for ways to promote consistency of treatment between home and school.*

» Reflect on the head teacher's statement as an example of how a primary school might help children to progress through the stage of heteronomy. Notice the emphasis on establishing simple rules and routines (moving from anomy to heteronomy) and on fostering independence in managing personal conduct (moving from heteronomy to autonomy). The school avoids any temptation to see a stage

> *theory as an excuse for waiting for children to pass naturally from one phase to the next, and obviously draws on Vygotsky's notion of scaffolding to ensure that progression is enhanced.*

Whereas the practical strategies recommended by Rogers and adopted in many schools have a basis in behaviourist psychology, it is important to notice that the objectives and underpinning aims found in schools' behaviour policies frequently draw also on constructivist principles. A judicious blending of the two approaches is likely to produce the best outcomes, for two reasons.

• Firstly, an approach derived solely from operant conditioning reduces behaviour management to something done to children, rather than involving them consciously in the process, whereas a strategy based solely on a constructivist policy ignores the importance of establishing the teacher's authority over the class. Combining the two enables you both to exert discipline in the classroom and also to help children to understand how to manage their conduct.

• Secondly, a teacher working only with a behaviourist perspective, though likely to succeed in imposing structure and order in the class, overlooks the task of nurturing children through building trusting and caring relationships with them. Conversely, one who seeks only to build positive relationships with the pupils downplays the need to gain ready compliance from the class. Again, a judicious combination of both strategies is ideal.

Canter's 2009 book, the fourth edition of a series of publications, argues cogently for this sort of approach, which seeks a balance between establishing a structured, disciplined classroom and building trusting and caring professional relationships with pupils. Canter's discussion of these contrasting, yet complementary factors evokes a striking recollection of the critique of Kohlberg's work offered by Gilligan (1977), who identified the importance of balancing moral discourse based on the concept of judgement with moral action predicated on the practice of compassion. The debate indicates that a key issue with which you will grapple as a teacher is the extent to which your dealings with pupils about their behaviour is led by your head or your heart. Canter's view, which is also very clearly reflected in the head teacher's statement above, is that both are vital, especially as pupils progress through the phase of heteronomy.

Moving towards moral autonomy

Becoming morally independent entails developing and internalising a set of principles, then acting in accordance with them. The acid test of the stage of autonomy involves behaving in this principled way at all times, not only when being observed by a figure of authority such as a parent or teacher. The concept of a personal conscience is obviously linked to this stage of personal development. If you ask two pupils how they know that stealing is wrong, one may say that someone who steals will get into trouble and the other that the stolen item is someone else's property and must not be taken from its owner. The first answer relates to the stage of heteronomy, since the moral arbiter is not the child but the person who will administer the punishment. The second reflects a child who possesses a moral belief about the intrinsic wrongness of stealing, and is thus entering the phase of autonomy, in Kohlberg's terms.

The importance of developing moral independence cannot be over-emphasised. People who remain stuck in the phase of heteronomy, and who continue to believe that the wrongness of an action lies in the fact that it leads to punishment, sooner or later draw the logical conclusion that if you are not caught and punished, the action cannot have been wrong. Significant numbers of those convicted by courts have an absence of moral independence; many also have poor language and number skills. On both counts, teachers can make a difference.

Since it is your role as a teacher to help children to move from stage to stage in their learning, it follows that you need a pedagogical repertoire to help pupils to become morally independent, in both their thinking and their behaviour. Your strategies should include techniques to aid moral reasoning and approaches designed to promote sensitivity to personal feelings, since situations involving moral choices often affect people's feelings as much as, if not more than, their reasoning faculties. Thus moral education must address both the cognitive and affective domains of learning.

Kohlberg asked his interviewees to discuss fictional situations which involved moral dilemmas. His purpose in doing so was to analyse their responses in order to gauge their level of moral reasoning. However, the same strategy can also be used to enable pupils to develop moral reasoning and insight, and to practise the skills of making moral judgements. McPhail et al. (1978) published sets of dilemmas based on situations reported to them by children in the middle years of schooling which made the children feel uncertain what to do. Using drama and role-play, along the lines advocated by Toye and Prendiville (1998), in working through the issues raised by moral dilemmas can enable children to explore moral situations within the safe environment afforded by a fictional context. The teacher's role in directing this type of work is necessarily sophisticated. In particular, you will wish to avoid the lesson resulting in children only saying what they think you will want to hear. You therefore need to adopt teaching strategies which indicate to the class that you are moving into role as a neutral chair of a debate. The children must be trained to understand that this gives them freedom to speak their minds, knowing that you will only intervene in the event of discriminatory, abusive or vulgar language. Likewise, you need to signal when you are coming out of role and resuming your customary authority as the teacher of the class. With practice, using this method with a class significantly enhances the relationship of mutual trust between teacher and pupils, as the following commentary from an experienced practitioner indicates.

REFLECTIVE TASK

Reflecting on alternative viewpoints

Teacher H has for several years been using moral dilemmas as a basis for debates, role-play and drama. He finds the approach invaluable as a stimulus for oral and written work in English, as well as fulfilling its intended purpose in moral development. Read his comments and reflect on the extent to which you might find his practice worth pursuing in your own teaching.

Teacher H: *In my career I've taught pupils from Y2 to Y8, because I've worked in middle schools as well as primaries. I stumbled across the potential of moral dilemmas by chance when I attended an RE course. At first I organised small group discussions around straightforward questions, for example, 'what should I do if I find a £10 note in the street?' Topics like that are useful, because they are realistic, and most of the issues that I used with my classes were suggested by the children themselves. It was important to train the children to understand that they could say whatever they liked, as long as they were sincere and polite, and that I would not be offended if their view was different from mine.*

I came to appreciate, however, that we were spending most of our time on theoretical discussions about moral judgements, and I wanted to get my pupils more involved with the emotional side of dilemmas. So I began to link my work on dilemmas with drama. The next year, I asked some of the children to develop a storyline based on a character who had been saving up to buy something costing £10, but had then lost the money on the way to the shops. They took turns at 'hotseating' this character, explaining to their classmates how they felt. The subsequent debate on the topic, 'what should I do if I find a £10 note in the street?' was totally different from previous occasions, because the children began to think about who might have lost the money, and what the loss might mean to them. Whereas previously the general conclusion had been that it was a lucky find, now there was a polarised debate about whether the finder should take the money to the police, or at least try to find the owner.

Another dilemma involved one child daring another to steal sweets from a shop, with a threat that, 'I won't be your friend if you don't do the dare'. The role-play associated with that storyline engaged a Y4 class in a discussion of the meaning of true friendship, and several children also spontaneously mentioned the potential loss to the shopkeeper. The interplay of intellectual and emotional responses is a very powerful component in this way of working. I think that is what stimulates the children in the oral and written work that accompanies the scenarios.

Notice how the teacher's final comment about the interplay of intellect and emotion picks up on Gillligan's (1977) discussion of Kohlberg's theories of moral development. Logical argument and sensitive insight are both part of moral discourse. The use of drama as an educational method helps children to integrate these two dimensions of their experience when dealing with moral issues.

In addition to structured teaching designed to foster moral autonomy, you can make productive use of the daily routines and practices of your classroom to enable children to experience being trusted to behave in desired ways. Distributing responsibilities around the class for the care and maintenance of apparatus and stock, taking messages to the office and setting out the classroom for the next activities are examples of how you can devolve some of your authority by sharing responsibility with children.

Learning behaviour and behaviour for learning

Chapter 5 discussed the importance of providing appropriately in the formal curriculum for children's different learning needs arising from their prior knowledge and skills. A comparable approach is needed when teaching pupils how to behave appropriately. It is not too far-fetched to think of behaviour as a curriculum area in its own right. Learning behaviour can be seen, alongside learning English and learning mathematics, as a core function of a school, as described by the head teacher of School X in the earlier reflective task.

Behaviour as an area of the curriculum

Parallels between learning behaviour and learning the formal curriculum subjects can clearly be described. Children's differing social and cultural settings will mean that they bring different experiences and understandings of acceptable conduct with them when they come to school, just as they bring different levels of literacy and numeracy. Some pupils will find the school's climate of values and required behaviour very similar to what is expected of them at home and in their communities. Others may encounter a significant mismatch between what is considered right and wrong in class and what they experience outside the school. Some of the sharpest contrasts relate to issues of equality. For example, some children may regularly hear discriminatory language about race, gender, sexual orientation or religion freely uttered at home and in wider society, or may be accustomed to hearing language liberally peppered with obscene or offensive words and expressions. Those children have more to learn about appropriate conduct in school than a child from a background where an inclusive philosophy is embraced and an avoidance of swearing is the norm.

The process described here is exactly parallel to the way in which good teachers operate in mathematics or any other formal subject. Proper account is taken of the diverse knowledge with which children arrive, then appropriately differentiated teaching and learning is planned. Those who need more support than others should be given it by varying the levels of scaffolding, to use Vygotsky's term. Prompt, constructive feedback from adults to children is as relevant when guiding behaviour as when teaching fractions.

Just as you will begin your lessons in language and mathematics by explaining your expectations and desired learning outcomes, so too you should make a point of telling children about the standards of behaviour that you expect. Jacques draws a valuable distinction between discipline and control (Jacques, 2007, p 125f), pointing out that 'discipline' is based on models of conduct agreed between teacher and pupils, whereas 'control' implies a more authoritarian style. Her helpful list of suggestions for managing day-to-day maintenance of good behaviour (p 126) is well worth considering.

REFLECTIVE TASK

Reflecting on your reading

Jacques, K (2007) Managing Challenging Behaviour, in Jacques, K and Hyland, R (eds) *Professional Studies: Primary and Early Years.* Third edition. Exeter: Learning Matters.

Read the list of suggestions set out in bold type on p 126 of this article. Use Jacques' ideas as an audit tool for your own practice. Reflect on situations that you have encountered when you made use of any of these strategies. Consider, too, times in your teaching experience that you could have handled more effectively in the light of these pointers.

Reflection on your personal response to children's conduct is also an important factor in helping children to learn behaviour. Eaude points out that the adult–child relationship is not a one-way process, but that particular incidents and individuals can provoke in adults strong emotional responses (Eaude, 2012, p 39). If unchecked, these can result in a worsening situation if the teacher responds inappropriately in front of the whole class. As the adult in the relationship, you must be prepared to modify your behaviours rather than always expecting children to alter theirs.

Managing behaviour to enable and promote learning

Self-reflection is also advocated by Adams in her discussion of behaviour for learning (Adams, 2011, p 225). She contends that adults, when in learning situations, often engage in behaviours that they would consider inappropriate if they were the tutor. It is consequently fruitless to expect perfection in children's behaviour, and a degree of compromise is needed in order to allow learning to take place.

It is certainly the case that all too many lessons have been disrupted because of teachers who constantly stopped the whole class to address an issue of behaviour pertaining to just a few pupils. This easily leads to a loss of pace and concentration as pupils (and teachers) lose the thread of the lesson. A well-paced lesson, with plenty of impetus and regular changes of focus, leaves less time for the sort of 'low level' disruptive behaviours identified in Ofsted reports as the most frequent type of misbehaviour. Ofsted has regularly reported on the close correlation between bad behaviour and poor teaching, pointing out that the converse is also true, namely that the best way to improve behaviour is through good teaching (Ofsted, 2013). It is certainly the case that many remedies for poor behaviour are within the competence of schools to implement. Adams rightly suggests that you can take many practical steps to prevent inappropriate behaviour by paying close attention to the preparation of the physical classroom environment. Your decisions about how children are to be seated, how they are to access resources and what they should do when they complete a task are vital. 'When children are unsure of what to do, you have unwittingly provided an opportunity for losing learning time at best, or engaging in disruptive behaviour at worst' (Adams, 2011, p 232).

Underpinning your work with the class you teach, there should be a range of different types of relationship. You need a class/teacher mode of operation, enabling you to address the class in a formal way as a large group. This is inevitably a relatively impersonal way of proceeding, but you need it particularly in beginning and ending lessons, at transition points, to make announcements about school routines and to deal decisively with sudden emergencies. In contrast, you should also develop an individual professional relationship with each child in the class. Being able to talk one-to-one about a child's hobbies and interests, their current home news and other significant events in their lives cements that type of relationship by demonstrating your active interest and concern for each pupil. Most children will not want to break this sort of bond, and your respect for them will engender their respect for you. Somewhere between these two modes of relationship comes the type of rapport you build with groups of pupils, for example when working with half a dozen pupils engaged in an activity during a lesson. Managing a group is clearly easier than controlling a whole class, so you can afford to be less formal and can become thoroughly immersed in the process of learning, alongside the children.

REFLECTIVE TASK

Reflecting on your teaching

Thinking about the class that you teach or have recently taught, run your eye down the class list. Reflect on what you know about each individual: their home circumstances, their interests, their hobbies, their friendships, favourite subjects, what they are currently reading.

» *Do you know more about some children than others? If so, why is that?*

» *Are some prominent because of challenging behaviour?*

» *Are some naturally 'loud' and others reticent or even withdrawn?*

» *Are any taken out of the classroom for learning support activities so often that you don't really know them?*

Your response to this task may suggest steps that you could helpfully take to ensure that all pupils benefit from a strong one-to-one professional relationship with you.

The notion of knowing your pupils individually is consistent with Weare's (2004) emphasis on the importance of emotional literacy. In her view, an emotionally literate school is one which takes seriously children's social and emotional contexts in understanding and guiding their behaviour. The approach is not without its hazards, as Ecclestone and Hayes (2009) point out, claiming that what they call 'therapeutic education' undermines pupils' resilience and risks turning them into self-preoccupied 'victims'. The key to charting an assured course between these two positions is to keep at the forefront of your mind the fact that your overriding purpose is children's education, and that includes teaching them to behave appropriately as well as teaching them the formal curriculum.

Performance of understanding

Thinking about the school in which you work or have recently worked, respond to the prompts after each intended learning outcome, as a means of identifying your knowledge and understanding of the issues covered in the chapter.

• *an understanding of the importance of rules and routines for behaviour in classrooms;*

- Identify the key rules and routines which operate in your school, and demonstrate how you have embedded them within your classroom practice and when moving with children around the school.

- Give a couple of examples showing how you have systematically referred to, and implemented, the school's rules and routines when giving rewards or sanctions to pupils for their behaviour.

- *confidence in your ability to promote good behaviour in the classroom and around the school;*

  - When attending an interview for a teaching post, how would you explain to the appointing panel your fundamental beliefs about, and key strategies for, fostering good behaviour in your classroom and around the school?

  - Identify ways in which you have entrusted children with opportunities to work independently or in groups without continuous direct supervision from you. How did you decide what level of responsibility to devolve to the pupils?

- *your knowledge of a range of strategies for managing pupils' behaviour, and an ability to use them consistently and effectively;*

  - Explain how you use praise and reward to acknowledge and reinforce good behaviour.

  - Identify occasions when you have made use of extrinsic and intrinsic motivation to underpin your strategies for behaviour management.

  - What approaches have you used successfully to address potentially disruptive behaviour in ways that did not lead to a hiatus in the processes of learning and teaching?

- *an understanding of ways of matching your behaviour management strategies to children's developmental needs;*

  - In the light of Vygotsky's assertion that children's differing social interactions outside school have a significant impact on their learning, give examples of occasions when you have deliberately differentiated the type of support that you give to individuals to help them in managing their own behaviour.

  - How is your approach to behaviour management related to the notion of a developmental continuum in children's moral understanding and behaviour?

- *an ability to form and maintain an appropriate teacher/pupil relationship with individuals, groups and classes.*

  - Explain, as if to an appointment panel, the different types of professional relationship that you have been able to form and maintain during your teaching to date.

  - Demonstrate by means of two or three examples how you have capitalised on your knowledge of individual pupils' personal interests to help them to improve their behaviour.

Taking it further

Behaviour4Learning. Available online at www.Behaviour4Learning.ac.uk (accessed 22 February 2014).

McLeod, S A (2011) *Kohlberg – Moral Development – Simply Psychology.* Available online at www. simplypsychology.org/kohlberg.html (accessed 15 November 2013).

Rogers, B (2006) *Classroom Behaviour: A Practical Guide to Effective Teaching, Behaviour Management and Colleague Support.* Third edition. London: Paul Chapman Publishing.

References

Adams, K (2009) *Behaviour for Learning in the Primary School.* Exeter: Learning Matters.

Adams, K (2011) Managing Behaviour for Learning, in Hansen, A (ed) *Primary Professional Studies.* Exeter: Learning Matters.

Benjamin, L T (2007) *A Brief History of Modern Psychology.* Oxford: Blackwell.

Canter, L (2009) *Assertive Discipline: Positive Behavior Management for Today's Classroom.* Fourth edition. Bloomington: Solution Tree.

Department of Education and Science (DES) (1988) *Education Reform Act, 1988.* London: HMSO.

Eaude, T (2012) *How Do Expert Primary Classteachers Really Work?* Northwich: Critical Publishing.

Ecclestone, K and Hayes, D (2009) *The Dangerous Rise of Therapeutic Education.* Abingdon: Routledge.

Ellis, S and Tod, J (2009) *Behaviour for Learning: Positive Approaches to Behaviour Management.* Abingdon: Routledge.

Ewens, T (2007) Spiritual, Moral, Social and Cultural Values in the Classroom, in Jacques, K and Hyland, R (eds) *Professional Studies: Primary and Early Years.* Third edition. Exeter: Learning Matters.

Gilligan, C (1977) In a Different Voice: Women's Conceptions of Self and of Morality. *Harvard Educational Review,* 47 (4): 481–517.

Hay/McBer Group (2000) *Research into Teacher Effectiveness: A Model of Teacher Effectiveness.* (DfEE Research Report 216). London: DfEE.

Jacques, K (2007) Managing Challenging Behaviour, in Jacques, K and Hyland, R (eds) *Professional Studies: Primary and Early Years.* Third edition. Exeter: Learning Matters.

Kohlberg, L (1984) *Essays on Moral Development, Vol.2, The Psychology of Moral Development.* San Francisco: Harper and Row.

McLeod, S A (2011) *Kohlberg – Moral Development – Simply Psychology.* Available online at www. simplypsychology.org/kohlberg.html (accessed 15 November 2013).

McPhail, D, Middleton, D and Ingram, D (1978) *Startline: Moral Education in the Middle Years.* (Schools Council Moral Education Project 8–13). London: Longman.

Murray, M E (2007) Moral Development and Moral Education – An Overview. University of Illinois. Available online at http://moodle.unitec.ac.nz/file.php/950/Day_9_childhood/MoralDevelopmentandMoralEducation.pdf (accessed 26 April 2014).

Office for Standards in Education (Ofsted) (2013) *The Report of Her Majesty's Chief Inspector of Education, Children's Services and Skills: Schools in 2012/13*. Available online at www.ofsted.gov.uk/resources/130236 (accessed 22.02.14).

Rogers, B (1998) *You Know the Fair Rule*. London: Prentice Hall.

Toye, N and Prendiville, F (1998) Drama as a Way to Teach Teachers about Teaching, in Richards, C, Simco, N and Twiselton, S (eds) *Primary Teacher Education: High Status? High Standards?* London: Falmer.

Weare, K (2004) *Developing the Emotionally Literate School*. London: Paul Chapman Publishing.

8 Fulfilling wider professional responsibilities

Learning outcomes

By the end of this chapter you should have developed and clarified:

- *an awareness of the school as a community and the roles that teachers can play in it;*

- *an understanding of ways in which staff members deploy specialist knowledge and skills to the benefit of their colleagues' work and pupils' learning;*

- *a knowledge of strategies for engaging support staff effectively and productively;*

- *an appreciation of professional development as an integral feature of a teacher's work; and*

- *an ability to communicate effectively with parents and carers.*

Many of the Teachers' Standards are predicated on the notion of a teacher working with a class of pupils. The eighth Standard, referring to wider professional responsibilities, raises questions about various contexts within which you work as a teacher. Your role in the staff room, your contribution to the general life of the school, your responsibilities to other members of the teaching profession, your duties towards members of the support staff and your relationship with parents, carers and volunteers are all examples of wider roles that teachers play.

Wider purposes of schools

A preoccupation in public discourse with the details of the formal curriculum (see Chapter 3) has drawn attention away from consideration of the overall aims of education, with the result that the broad views of a school's purposes illustrated in vision statements or mission statements sit uneasily alongside the requirement to teach a defined group of subjects. Yet a stated aim of education, which has remained little changed in legislation in England, is the requirement dating from the 1944 Education Act that the education service should promote 'the spiritual, moral, mental and physical development of the community'. In a recent formulation (DfE, 2013a), it appears as follows:

Every state-funded school must offer a curriculum which is balanced and broadly based and which:

- promotes the spiritual, moral, cultural, mental and physical development of pupils at the school and of society; and

- prepares pupils at the school for the opportunities, responsibilities and experiences of later life.

(DfE 2013a, p 5)

These statements presuppose that schools will have a 'wider life': wider, that is, than the teaching of a named curriculum.

In preparing for the 2014 version of the national curriculum, the following statement was produced by the Department for Education (DfE):

The National Curriculum has three aims. It should enable all young people to become:

- *successful learners who enjoy learning, make progress and achieve*

- *confident individuals who are able to live safe, healthy and fulfilling lives*

- *responsible citizens who make a positive contribution to society.*

(DfE, 2013b)

Although set out as functions of the curriculum, these statements are really aims of education and, as such, it is important to look well beyond the formal curriculum when thinking about how they are to be achieved. This is why schools typically refer to themselves as communities, or as providing certain types of environment, when setting out their visions or missions. There is also a connection with the 'informal curriculum' and the 'hidden curriculum' (see Chapter 5), both of which are aspects of your work in school which help to shape children's spiritual, moral, social and cultural identities in a way that contributes to the achievement of the aims promoted in the DfE statement. It is unfortunate that the word 'curriculum' has been so overworked in educational debate that it has obscured discussion of the broader purposes of schooling.

REFLECTIVE TASK

Reflecting on your reading

Qualifications and Curriculum Authority (QCA) (2013) *The Aims of the Curriculum*.

Read this short paper, which provides desirable outcomes by way of exemplification for each of the three aims of the national curriculum set out by the DfE.

»   *To what extent do you agree with each of the objectives offered by the QCA in support of the three aims?*

> » *Can you identify other desirable outcomes arising from the aims, that are not specified in the paper?*

Select a couple of statements from each of the three lists set out in the QCA paper. Reflect on some of the ways in which a school might enable its pupils to achieve the outcomes.

> » *To what degree do you think the formal subjects of the national curriculum contribute to the process?*

> » *What other aspects of school life do you consider can make a telling or decisive contribution?*

School as community

Redding (1991, p 8) comments aptly that 'teachers are not isolated practitioners of pedagogy, but professionals integrated into the web of community and buoyed by common purpose'. Schools' vision statements or mission statements often indicate that they see themselves as communities (see examples quoted in Chapter 9) based on sets of shared values which underpin everything that takes place within the organisation. From a pupil's perspective, the school's communal values are often communicated during collective worship, still described in some schools as 'assembly'. In fact, both terms ought to have currency since, in addition to meeting the requirement to provide a daily act of collective worship, an assembly of the whole school, or of groups within the school, provides an ideal opportunity to convey messages about the values that the school professes in its vision statement, and to celebrate examples showing those values in practice.

Several of the exemplification statements from the QCA paper are typically addressed by schools at 'assembly' time, often but not invariably related to material presented during collective worship, for example the aspirations that children should:

* have secure values and beliefs and have principles to distinguish right from wrong;

* respect others and act with integrity;

* understand their own and others' cultures and traditions;

* appreciate the benefits of diversity;

* challenge injustice, be committed to human rights and strive to live peaceably with others.

REFLECTIVE TASKS

Reflecting on alternative viewpoints

A group of French trainee teachers on an exchange visit to an English university visited several schools. Asked what distinguished English primary education from French schooling they unanimously identified 'l'esprit de l'école', the spirit of the school, which they judged was shaped by what happened at assembly time. The opportunity for the head teacher and other staff members to articulate a common philosophy was thought by them to be a crucial factor in establishing the climate of expected relationships and conduct. One commented, 'of course it would be important that all staff members were generally in agreement with the philosophy, so that the principles expressed during the assembly could also be upheld during lessons and at break times'.

» *In the light of these comments, identify ways in which you have become aware of the philosophical and/or religious values espoused in your school.*

» *Do you agree with the French trainee teachers about the crucial role played by assemblies and collective worship in establishing a climate of values?*

Reflecting on your own schooldays

Identify some of the features of collective worship and/or assemblies that you experienced as a primary school pupil.

» *To what extent can you identify with the remarks of the French trainee teachers reported in the above example?*

» *Do you recognise their claim that these occasions were key opportunities for the school's values to be promoted and celebrated?*

» *Was there continuity between what happened in assemblies and the life of your classroom?*

» *How might reflecting on experiences as a former pupil shape your own views about good practice?*

Implicit in this discussion is the notion that you have a role to play in helping to determine your school's philosophy and ethos, for example through your contributions to formal discussions in staff meetings and informal conversations in the staff room. You also have a duty to uphold the school's declared values when working with your class, supervising break time, taking an after-school club or leading an educational visit. To some extent this is a matter of implementing agreed procedures set out in the staff handbook. But underpinning these procedures is – or should be – an ethos based on clear statements of value. For the children there is something to be gained from being taught by adults who differ from one another to some extent in their beliefs and attitudes. But such differences can become a negative influence if they appear to undermine the school's core values. For that reason it is important, when applying for posts, to investigate whether you can give your commitment to the values set out in the school's publicity.

Aside from whole-school gatherings and the life of the staff room, other possible ways in which you may contribute to the community of the school include running informal clubs, assisting with arts activities or sports, engaging in educational visits including residential opportunities, serving on the Parent–Teachers' Association, acting as an elected staff governor and using specialist knowledge by leading colleagues, an issue explored in detail later in the chapter.

Your classroom is a further example of a community, functioning as a sub-set of the whole school community. Implications of this are considered in Chapter 7.

Kerridge and Sayers (2006) summarise a sociological analysis of the term 'community' under three headings:

1. physical proximity, referring to those living in a neighbourhood;

2. civic identity, as in people with shared characteristics but scattered around an area, for example the Polish, Welsh-speaking or Roman Catholic communities;

3. collective identity, referring to groups based on a common purpose or interest, such as a workplace or a sports club.

A school is an example of the third of these types, but in all probability it also serves communities of both the other sorts. Ewens (2011, pp 151–53) provides a case study offering a pen portrait of what this can mean in practice. The 'wider life and ethos of the school' referred to in Standard 8 could be expressed in two different ways when considering the school's relationship to the wider community:

*   activities designed to benefit members of the community beyond the pupil population;

*   activities designed to enrich the pupils' curriculum by using the community as an object of study.

These two approaches relate to the second and third of three constructs identified by Redding (1991):

1. the school as a community;

2. the school in the community; and

3. the school and the community.

A school which sees itself as 'in the community' might for example offer adult education classes in English as an additional language, open its facilities to youth groups and sports clubs and liaise with other providers to locate IT training for adults into a programme of evening classes. In certain circumstances it might see itself as the hub for multi-service provision in the neighbourhood, so that local residents could access health and social services on site. Voyles (2012) sketches such an initiative in a small town in America, noting that the resulting social benefit appeared to have led to gains in educational achievement among the pupils at the school. While you may well have no front-line role in initiatives of this sort, you are well placed to advertise and commend the provision to parents and carers.

A focus on the school 'and the community' enables the curriculum to be significantly enhanced by incorporating ways of using local communities within the children's regular programme of learning. Your class might for example learn at first hand about people, buildings and activities situated close to the school in order to find out about the businesses and services that enable society to function, as well as exploring the locality's historical, religious and cultural infrastructure. There is a balance to be struck between taking children out into the community and inviting community members to visit the school to work with the children. In either event, there are important issues to be addressed to ensure pupils' welfare and safety, but it is usually well worth the effort of undertaking your school's appropriate procedures for educational visits or for inviting a visitor to school.

The benefit of linking school and community in the curriculum is not restricted to local communities. Once children have grasped the concept of community, and what it means to belong to one, they have a powerful model for investigating distant communities as well, using a 'compare and contrast' approach.

Collegiality

The concept of collegiality is illuminated by the Latin root of the word, which means 'bound together'. Colleagues are thus people who are bound together in a shared enterprise, forming a community of expertise. It is consequently vital to establish good professional relationships within the group of staff members, in order to maximise the efficiency and success of the school. Different types of interaction are apparent, depending on the sort of activity being undertaken.

Co-operation and collaboration among teachers

Sometimes your work with colleagues is on a shared and equal footing. A typical example is when the teachers of parallel classes in a year group co-operate to plan the medium-term curriculum, to monitor progress and to evaluate previous work. Unless the school is so large that there is a named year leader the teachers concerned operate as a group of equals, each contributing ideas, experiences and resources to the discussion, and sharing tasks among them.

Virtually all primary schools have nominated teachers who take the lead in certain areas of the curriculum. Since the Primary Survey of 1978 (HMI, 1978) primary schools have been encouraged to deploy teachers' specialist knowledge for the benefit of their colleagues, without fundamentally changing the notion of the generalist class teacher. The early vision, that there would be a teacher to lead each area of the curriculum, is practically unattainable for two reasons:

- firstly, there are very many schools with too few pupils to support a staff large enough to cover the entire curriculum;

- secondly, the areas of expertise among primary teachers are not equally distributed. For example, there is a comparative dearth of mathematics and science specialists but plenty of teachers with expertise in arts and humanities subjects.

However, given a willingness to undertake professional development in a non-specialist area, many teachers have become excellent leaders in areas of the curriculum that they did not initially regard as strengths. In part, this process has been facilitated by the insight that the extent of pure subject knowledge required of a successful primary teacher is perhaps of less importance than a grasp of pedagogical subject knowledge (see Chapter 3). Other roles in which teachers commonly lead their colleagues include that of SENDCO (Special Educational

Needs and Disabilities Co-ordinator), pastoral responsibilities, outdoor education as the EVC (Educational Visits Co-ordinator) and, in very large schools, year leadership.

Although sometimes described as 'distributed leadership', this way of sharing responsibilities among colleagues is perhaps more appropriately defined as 'delegated leadership', in the light of Storey's (2004) discussion of the concept of distributed leadership. Ultimately the head teacher is responsible for what happens in school, but his or her management role is most effectively discharged when specific responsibilities are devolved to others who have specialist knowledge and training.

Curriculum leadership

You will certainly be involved in the process of curriculum leadership. Even if you do not presently hold a responsibility for leading an area of the curriculum, many of your colleagues will do so, and you need to be responsive to their leadership. Since the 1978 Primary Review (HMI, 1978), the role description of a curriculum leader has developed significantly. Initially, there was resistance to the idea, as it was seen by some as an intrusion into personal professional practice, but the notion of whole-school curriculum planning and teaching gradually gained acceptance. At first, many curriculum co-ordinators did little more than maintain the stock of resources for the subject. However, in some subjects, notably music and PE, they were sometimes involved in teaching the subject throughout the school, often to the detriment of their own classes, which were taught by a succession of teachers released in the process.

Bell and Ritchie (1999), Dean (2003) and Burton and Brundrett (2005) all track developments in the concept and practice of curriculum leadership since the 1978 Primary Review, not least in nomenclature. The term curriculum co-ordinator was supplanted by 'subject leader' in the 1990s and later 'curriculum leader', reflecting changes in official views of the primary curriculum. Currently, teachers holding responsibility for an area of the curriculum are likely to be engaged in some, if not all, of the following activities with regard to their area:

- overseeing the school policy and scheme of work;
- contributing to cross-curricular planning, for example with regard to the use of language and number throughout the curriculum;
- maintaining and updating subject-specific resources, apparatus and equipment;
- keeping abreast of current developments, nationally and locally;
- leading staff development and training;
- liaising with colleagues in other schools;
- monitoring teaching and assessment throughout the school, and giving feedback to colleagues;
- reporting to the head teacher and other senior managers;
- contributing to the performance management of colleagues;
- making presentations to the school's governing body;
- briefing support staff, volunteer helpers and parents and carers.

Although you might initially think of the curriculum leader's remit as essentially a management role, the reality is more complex, as the following reflective tasks indicate:

REFLECTIVE TASKS

Reflecting on alternative viewpoints

Read these contributions from experienced teachers, reporting on their work as curriculum leaders. Thinking about the area of the curriculum that you find hardest to teach, reflect on how a specialist colleague could best help you to develop your knowledge and skills in that subject.

Teacher S: *In my first year of teaching I became the co-ordinator for Design Technology in a one-form entry primary school, as I had specialised in it during my initial teacher education. At the outset I provided lots of information and plans for my colleagues, but they seemed reluctant to use my ideas. When I thought about it, I realised that all the other teachers were quite a lot older than me, and had been trained before technology became part of the primary curriculum. On looking at what they were doing in their classrooms, I noticed that most of the work was very didactic in character. The children were being told about technology without being given opportunities to work with materials, find out about their properties, and try to design and make solutions to problems. I discussed my findings with the head, who encouraged me to think about my curriculum leadership role as that of a teacher trainer. We decided to organise a training session for one half of a teacher day, and I set up a workshop of practical activities for my colleagues to try for themselves. That was a turning point. Most of them got the point of the exercise and, over the next couple of years, I had lots of one-to-one discussions with individual colleagues about the activities that they undertook with their classes, and people were happy to talk about the subject in the staff room. Gradually this changed the pedagogy of the subject through the school.*

Teacher T: *I think what you're saying is that being a curriculum leader is more like being an adult education tutor than being a manager. You can only do the managerial roles, like writing schemes of work and monitoring the teaching of your subject throughout the school once your colleagues have a shared understanding of what is required, and have developed the knowledge and skills needed to tackle the subject with their own classes.*

Reflecting on your teaching

Identify a different area of the curriculum that you find challenging to teach. Reflect on the ways in which your understanding, knowledge and skills in that subject have developed during a period of teaching. To what extent have any of the following been of value?

*   reading the school policy and scheme of work.

*   observing an experienced teacher with some expertise in the subject.

*   undertaking private study and investigation.

- co-teaching with the curriculum leader or another experienced colleague.
- receiving advice and feedback from another colleague?

» *How comfortable are you with the notion of asking for advice and support from another teacher?*

It would be easy to think that each individual teacher ought to be able to demonstrate mastery of all the Standards unaided. After all, traditional approaches to assessment envisage that it is the independent performance of each candidate that should be examined. While it is true that every teacher needs to demonstrate competence in the classroom, it is also the case that teachers develop their repertoire of expertise most readily in the context of a collaborative network of professionals. This is a strong argument for a staffing structure which combines the traditional relationship between one teacher and a class with approaches which draw upon teachers' specialist knowledge and skills as well as their generalist abilities. The model of curriculum leadership reflected in the reflective tasks described above is predicated on the view that curriculum leaders can enable their colleagues to develop their ability to teach with increasing expertise across the breadth of the curriculum. A complementary model emphasises the desirability of introducing specialist teaching in primary schools, at least in upper Key Stage 2.

Specialist teaching

The *Cambridge Primary Review* (Alexander, 2010a) argued strongly for a reconsideration of the reliance on class teachers as the mainstay of the staffing structures in primary schools. Whereas that approach was appropriate in earlier generations, when the curriculum was much narrower, the demands made on individual teachers' subject knowledge nowadays are, Alexander claims, impossible to meet, especially in upper Key Stage 2. Your wider responsibility towards your colleagues in respect of areas in which you have expertise may therefore in future involve teaching their classes for your specialist areas, as well as acting as a curriculum leader for generalist colleagues.

REFLECTIVE TASK

Reflecting on your reading

Read the section 'Call in the Specialists?' from Alexander's Introduction to the *Cambridge Primary Review* (Alexander, 2010b, pp 36–38), in which he contends that:

> *Subject expertise is so crucial to educational quality that it challenges primary teachers' professional identity as generalists. If that challenge is ignored, the Review's definition of curriculum entitlement as the highest possible standards of teaching in all domains, regardless of time allocated, will remain a pipe dream.*
> (Alexander, 2010b, p 37)

» *Consider carefully the arguments with which Alexander supports this claim, and reflect on the areas of the curriculum in which you think you could offer specialist or semi-specialist teaching.*

> »   *What would be the implications for the school in which you teach, or recently taught,*
> *if the Review's proposals were to be implemented?*

It would be easy to dismiss the Review's proposal as impracticable, for the reasons given earlier in the chapter when discussing curriculum leadership. Very many schools are too small to have enough staff to offer specialist teaching, and in most the balance of expertise would not be ideal. Further, some teachers with specialist skills would be those who are class teachers in Key Stage 1, and the case for removing them to teach various Key Stage 2 classes is weakened by a consideration of the consequences for their own classes.

You may be working in a school which relies on a network of curriculum leaders to support generalist class teaching, or in a school where subject specialist teaching is practised to some extent. If your school is involved in a federation with other schools, or in a looser cluster arrangement, you may find that expertise is shared across the schools, so that children benefit from specialist expertise of staff from other settings. Whatever the model followed in your school, it is certain that you will be expected to respond to the leadership and guidance of other teachers, and also to make your own contribution as a teacher of teachers in a role agreed between you and your head teacher.

Leadership of a classroom team

The type of collegiality discussed in the previous section viewed a staff team as an interrelated network of professionals, offering mutual support to one another. A very different notion of collegiality applies within your classroom if you are the teacher with ultimate responsibility for a class of children. In this case, you are accountable for what happens in the class, and consequently you are the leader of a classroom team. Other team members may be Teaching Assistants (TAs), trainee teachers or volunteer helpers.

Blatchford et al. (2012) report the findings of the DISS (Deployment and Impact of Support Staff) project, a large and detailed study, which showed that despite a huge increase in the number of TAs working in English classrooms, their overall impact on pupil performance was often negative. This contradicted the positive views expressed by teachers about TAs' impact. Since the expansion in TA numbers most frequently resulted from Local Authority decisions to use them to support pupils with Special Educational Needs (SEN), this finding was particularly concerning.

REFLECTIVE TASK

Reflecting on your reading

Read the vignette on pages 1–5 of Blatchford et al. (2012) *Reassessing the Impact of Teaching Assistants*. Identify the factors that might have led the class teacher 'Mark' and the TA 'Mandy' to judge that their provision for the pupil 'Reece' was beneficial to him.

> » *From the researcher's description of what was actually happening in the classroom, can you list factors which might have led to the conclusion of the DISS project that 'relative to other pupils who received little or no TA support, the more support pupils like Reece received from TAs, the less progress they made in English, maths and science over a school year' (p 5)?*

This is a very worrying finding, not least because TAs now form about one-third of the primary school workforce, and it is vital that, as the lead professional in your classroom, you should understand how to avoid the negative outcomes found in the DISS study, and capitalise on the potential benefits of working with TAs and other adults in the classroom.

Prominent among the issues revealed in the DISS report that you need to address are:

* unquestioned assumptions that simply having additional adults in the classroom will necessarily bring about educational improvements;

* ensuring that you and the TA focus on educational achievement rather than task completion;

* being sure that the TA has subject knowledge and pedagogical subject knowledge relevant to the lesson;

* finding ways of sharing your planning, and your intended learning outcomes, with the TA;

* making sure that all pupils in the class have quality contact with you, the class teacher, and that no individuals or groups operate in such a way that they seldom work with the class teacher.

Following their work on the DISS project, the same authors undertook the EDTA (Effective Deployment of Teaching Assistants) project, in which they developed a 'Wider Pedagogical Role' model as the basis for enhancing the value of TAs' work. The results, published in Russell et al. (2013), emphasise three features as crucial to effective work by TAs:

1. training for both TAs and teachers, for the former in subject and pedagogical knowledge, for the latter in making the most of their TAs, and allocation of planning and preparation (PPA) time together;

2. deployment of TAs by head teachers and teachers; and

3. focus on the nature and quality of TAs' interactions with pupils.

Prior to the DISS and EDTA projects, no large-scale research into TAs' effectiveness had been conducted. While there had been small-scale studies identifying examples of good practice (eg Vincett et al., 2005), these had not been brought into mainstream thinking. The legacy of the DISS and EDTA studies is reflected in the exemplification statement under Standard 8, requiring you to deploy support staff effectively.

Many of the issues raised in connection with leading support staff effectively apply also to the deployment of volunteers helping in your class. If you are a fairly recently qualified teacher, you also have to take account of the fact that those supporting you may be senior to you in age and experience. Nevertheless, as the qualified teacher, you are the appointed team leader.

Maintaining and enhancing your knowledge and skills

The preamble to the Teachers' Standards asserts that teachers 'keep their knowledge and skills as teachers up-to-date and are self-critical'. This statement emphasises that professional development is a career-long aspect of your work, and that the time you spend as a trainee teacher accounts for only part of your professional education. Eady (2011) makes it clear that personal professional development 'is not something "done *to* you" but something "done *by* you" ultimately to support children's learning and development' (p 167). This definition places your continuing professional development (CPD) at the heart of what it means to be a reflective primary teacher, since the aim of reflective practice is the improvement of performance, and a self-critical disposition can assist in this.

Determining your CPD needs is a sophisticated process. One key approach is to identify issues arising from your practice which raise questions for you about how to proceed. For example, as a result of discussion with a mentor or other senior colleague, you may decide to focus on an aspect of behaviour management, a pedagogical topic or an assessment issue. Another approach results from external decisions, for example a government-sponsored initiative which requires teachers to learn new knowledge and skills. The head teacher's responsibilities include balancing your individual aspirations on the one hand with the institution's imperatives based on the school's improvement plan or a national strategy on the other hand. Sometimes this can create a tension, if individual teachers' needs do not fit readily with school priorities, as the following task illustrates.

REFLECTIVE TASK

Reflecting on alternative viewpoints

Consider this conversation between head teacher P, a recently appointed head, and her more experienced colleague Q, as they discuss the management of CPD. Given that head teachers have to take difficult decisions about the allocation of staff time and the CPD budget, what can you learn from this discussion about the politics of CPD planning?

Head teacher P: *Our recent Ofsted inspection identified a weakness in writing, especially among boys, so we've had to completely alter our plans for CPD throughout the school. Sadly that means that I've had to tell our NQT (Newly Qualified Teacher) that her plans to extend her work on art across the curriculum have to be put on hold. She's understandably upset, but we have to put the children's best interests ahead of the staff's.*

Head teacher Q: *Could I put a different slant on the issue? Our art co-ordinator is attending the same course as your NQT, and he thinks there will be real benefits to children's oral and written work from some of the suggestions arising from the course. You don't always improve writing just by concentrating on writing. Sometimes it's a case of providing children with a stimulus that makes them want to convey their ideas. Since your NQT is passionate about art, it might be worth backing her CPD request, with the proviso that she should look out especially for links between art and writing.*

Pedder et al. (2009) found that effective professional development, especially in the early years of teaching, tended to be based on classroom practice and to involve personal reflection together with feedback, coaching and mentoring from more experienced colleagues. Outcomes were more likely to be positive, in terms of benefits to pupils' learning, when teachers had themselves been involved in needs identification. Just as expert teachers often allow children to take the lead in their own learning, so experienced head teachers can enable teachers to lead the way in CPD, and harness the resulting energy to an identified need of the school. Conversely, in schools with low achievement levels or poor inspection outcomes, the programme of CPD is likely to be structured around whole-school targets, often restricted to improving literacy and numeracy. Head teacher Q's philosophy is a direct challenge to such a mechanistic response.

You may find it helpful to think of your CPD activity under three headings:

1. using critical reflection as the basis for improvement in your day-to-day teaching. This is most likely to be fruitful if you can identify very specific focal points, for example 'transitions during science lessons' or 'liaising with the TA during lessons';

2. participating in school-wide CPD. This brings benefits in terms of collaboration with colleagues towards shared goals identified by the head and endorsed by the governing body;

3. pursuing longer-term aspirations. Your career plans may be best advanced by undertaking structured CPD over a period of time. Eady (2011, pp 170–78) outlines various opportunities for accredited CPD, for example leading to Master's qualifications, and almost invariably designed such that participants investigate their own practice in the light of theoretical perspectives.

Enlightened head teachers perceive one of their roles as being to move teachers on in their practice and in their careers, and take pride in helping staff members to gain promotion, since a constant, measured turnover of staff can be very healthy for a school. For this reason, you should not hesitate to maintain a conversation with your head teacher and other senior colleagues about your perceived CPD needs and ambitions.

Communicating effectively with parents and carers

Your duty to parents and carers includes a requirement to provide a written report at least annually and to attend parents' evenings to discuss children's work, progress and well-being. Good communication between teachers and parents is clearly desirable, and these formal requirements are designed to ensure that parents are kept informed about their children's achievements at school. There are some obvious pitfalls to be negotiated. One is to ensure that your written and oral comments are not couched in educational jargon to the extent that parents are mystified. On the other hand, you must at all costs avoid appearing to patronise parents by an over-simplistic report. Part of the school's task is to help parents to understand the current arrangements for the curriculum and assessment, so the use of vocabulary about Key Stages and levels of attainment are usually appropriate. Another issue is that of confidentiality. For instance, at a parents' evening, if you are asked whether a particular child is performing better than his or her friend, you must at all costs maintain professional confidentiality and confine your comments to that parent's child. However, it would be entirely proper to discuss the child's attainment in relation to the nationally expected level of performance for the age group.

Most teachers would accept that, for communication between teacher and parent to be really effective, there need to be opportunities for less formal contact other than at parents' evenings. A good professional teacher/parent relationship ought to allow for a two-way exchange of information. For example, it can be invaluable for the teacher to be made aware of major disruptions to the child's home life such as bereavement or a broken relationship, since these may well affect a child's performance. In any case, the teacher will wish to avoid insensitivity in daily conversation with children, so awareness of difficult issues is important. Parents are more likely to disclose such information in the context of a trusting relationship, in which they can count on you to treat what they tell you in a professional manner.

Hayes (2012) includes in Part 2 of his book some valuable insights into parent/teacher relationships, while Ellicott (2013) offers a comment following the publication of test results suggesting that English pupils' attainment at 15 lags far behind that of Chinese pupils.

The following extracts describe different approaches to sustaining teacher/parent links:

REFLECTIVE TASK

Reflecting on alternative viewpoints

Consider the points made by the following members of staff about communicating with parents.

»   *Do you agree with them?*

»   *To what extent do they mirror practice in the school in which you teach, or have recently taught?*

Teacher A: *I teach a Reception/Year 1 class and make a point of being available to parents at the classroom door at the beginning and end of the day. My teaching assistant deals very ably with settling the children when they arrive, and she makes sure that they are ready for registration in the morning and that they leave with the correct person in the evening. A brief word with a parent before school starts or ends allows us to update one another about issues that may affect a child's behaviour or learning. If we need longer we make an appointment for a private conversation at another time.*

Teacher B: *I agree that parents and teachers need to be on the same wavelength, and this can be difficult if children attend breakfast club or after-school club, since I tend not to meet the parents other than at parents' evenings. In my Year 2 class each child has a notebook to take home with their reading book and any other homework tasks. The parents and I (and sometimes grandparents and older siblings) use it to correspond with one another. Usually this is about the child's progress, but sometimes we use it to pass on other information or to raise concerns about any topic. If necessary we arrange to meet or to speak on the phone.*

Teacher C: *My class is Year 6, so parents are unlikely to visit on a daily basis. Our junior department makes use of the school website to keep parents informed about the curriculum. Sometimes this results in a parent with specialised knowledge making a contribution to a project. As a school, we make use of text and e-mail communication with parents, but also send a hard copy weekly newsletter home. We make a point of having a parents' evening very early in the Autumn Term. This gives a useful opportunity to make face-to-face contact with parents about individual pupils, and we emphasise that we are always prepared to meet them individually to discuss difficulties.*

Head teacher X: *Each child only has one shot at education, so good communication with parents is vital. However, it's important to balance that so that teachers are not excessively deflected from the key task of teaching the class. Over the years I've found that a parents' evening early in the year, together with clear information online and in regular newsletters, reassures most parents that our staff are doing their very best for the children. The most intractable problem concerns those parents who never attend parents' evenings; invariably they are the ones that teachers feel they most need to see.*

As with other areas of the Standards, the examples considered here demonstrate that good practitioners go well beyond the basic requirements in fulfilling their professional obligations.

Performance of understanding

Thinking about the school in which you work or have recently worked, respond to the prompts after each intended learning outcome, as a means of identifying your knowledge and understanding of the issues covered in the chapter.

- *an awareness of the school as a community and the roles that teachers can play in it;*

    - Identify from the school's website or prospectus the ways it describes itself as a community. What are the main values that it sets out as core to its vision?

    - Reflecting on your recent teaching, identify some examples of ways in which you shared with, or portrayed to, your class one or more of the core values of the school community.

    - What contributions do you make to the wider life and ethos of your school, beyond your classroom?

- Identify one or two instances in which you have drawn upon the local community of people and places to enrich children's learning.

- *an understanding of ways in which staff members deploy specialist knowledge and skills to the benefit of their colleagues' work and pupils' learning;*

  - Select an area of the curriculum in which you feel less confident to teach. Identify the colleague best placed to offer information and advice, and find out what support they can provide for you.

  - What are the arrangements in the school for supporting pupils with SEND?

  - Identify from the staff handbook the members of staff with responsibilities for areas of the curriculum, pastoral matters, educational visits and child protection.

- *a knowledge of strategies for engaging support staff effectively and productively;*

  - From your recent planning identify a lesson in which a TA was supporting you. Analyse the session to identify how you ensured that the TA appreciated the intended learning outcomes and had appropriate subject and pedagogical knowledge.

  - How do you monitor the learning and progress of groups and individuals in sessions in which they are working with a TA or a volunteer?

- *an appreciation of professional development as an integral feature of a teacher's work;*

  - In what ways do you build into your professional routines a mechanism for identifying topics to study and reflect on, as a means of generating your own CPD?

  - What can you gain from, and contribute to, your school's current programme of CPD?

  - What longer-term plans do you have for the development of your career, and what are the implications for your personal CPD programme?

- *an ability to communicate effectively with parents and carers.*

  - Select three children from your class and reflect on how you would report to their parents on their progress, achievements and effort. How can you be informative without using technical language which may obscure, rather than illuminate, a true picture?

  - Looking at the class register, identify those parents you think you know reasonably well, those whom you have met once or twice, and those whom you have never met. Do any patterns emerge from this exercise? Consider whether there are other strategies that you might use.

Taking if further

Alexander, R (ed) (2010b) *Introducing the Cambridge Primary Review*. Available online at www.primaryreview.org.uk/downloads/Finalreport/CPR-booklet_low-res.pdf (accessed 30 November 2013).

Eady, S (2011) Personal Professional Development, in Hansen, A (ed) *Primary Professional Studies*. Exeter: Learning Matters.

Fraser, C and Meadows, S (2008) Children's Views of Teaching Assistants in Primary Schools. *Education 3–13*, 36 (4): 351–63.

Hancock, R and Collins, J (2012) *Primary Teaching Assistants: Learners and Learning*. Second edition. London: David Fulton.

References

Alexander, R (ed) (2010a) *Children, Their World, Their Education: Final Report and Recommendations of the Cambridge Primary Review*. Abingdon: Routledge.

Alexander, R (ed) (2010b) *Introducing the Cambridge Primary Review*. Available online at www.primaryreview.org.uk/downloads/Finalreport/CPR-booklet_low-res.pdf (accessed 30 November 2013).

Bell, D and Ritchie, R (1999) *Towards Effective Subject Leadership in The Primary School*. Buckingham: Open University Press.

Blatchford, P, Russell, A and Webster, R (2012) *Reassessing the Impact of Teaching Assistants*. Abingdon: Routledge.

Burton, N and Brundrett, M (2005) *Leading the Curriculum in the Primary School*. London: Paul Chapman Publishing.

Dean, J (2003) *Subject Leadership in the Primary School*. Abingdon: David Fulton.

Department for Education (DfE) (2013a) *The National Curriculum in England: Framework Document for Consultation*. London: DfE.

Department for Education (DfE) (2013b) *Aims, Values and Purposes*. Available online at www.education.gov.uk/schools/teachingandlearning/curriculum/b00199676/aims-values-and-purposes/aims (accessed 28 November 2013).

Eady, S (2011) Personal Professional Development, in Hansen, A (ed) *Primary Professional Studies*. Exeter: Learning Matters.

Ellicott, C (2013) The Secret of China's Schooling Success? Pushy Parents and Even Pushier Teachers. *Mail Online,* 4 December 2013.

Ewens, T (2011) The School Community: Being Part of a Wider Professional Environment, in Hansen, A (ed) *Primary Professional Studies*. Exeter: Learning Matters.

Hayes, D (2012) *Foundations of Primary Teaching*. Fifth Edition. Abingdon: Routledge.

Her Majesty's Inspectors (HMI) (1978) *Primary Education in England*. London: HMSO.

Kerridge, V and Sayers, R (2006) Community Education: Innovation and Active Intervention, in Sharp, J, Ward, S and Hankin, L (eds) *Education Studies: An Issues-Based Approach*. Exeter: Learning Matters.

Pedder, D, Storey, A and Opfer, D (2009) *Schools and Continuing Professional Development in England: The State of the Nation, Synthesis Report*. London: Training and Development Agency.

Qualifications and Curriculum Authority (QCA) (2013) *The Aims of the Curriculum*. Available online at www.media.education.gov.uk/assets/files/pdf/c/curriculum%20aims.pdf (accessed 28 November 2013).

Redding, S (1991) What is a School Community, Anyway? *The School Community Journal*, 1 (2): 7–9. Lincoln, IL: Academic Development Institute.

Russell, A, Webster, R and Blatchford, P (2013) *Maximising the Impact of Teaching Assistants: Guidance for School Leaders and Teachers*. Abingdon: Routledge.

Storey, A (2004) The Problem of Distributed Leadership in Schools. *School Leadership and Management*, 24 (3) Abingdon: Routledge

Vincett, K, Cremin, H and Thomas, G (2005) *Teachers and Assistants Working Together*. Maidenhead: Open University Press.

Voyles, M M (2012) Perceived Needs of At-Risk Families in a Small Town. *The School Community Journal*, 22 (2): 31–64. Lincoln, IL: Academic Development Institute.

9 Personal and professional conduct

Learning outcomes

By the end of this chapter you should have developed and clarified:

* *an appreciation of the concept of a profession and what makes teaching a profession;*

* *some insights into the relationship between personal conduct and professional responsibility;*

* *knowledge of professional and legal frameworks within which teachers operate; and*

* *your awareness of the professional knowledge, understanding, skills and attitudes which teachers must display.*

Part Two of the Standards contains just one standard: Personal and Professional Conduct. However, any suggestion that this aspect of your work can be isolated from everything else that you do is quickly dispelled when you read the bulleted statements which exemplify this section of the Standards. High levels of conduct, in both moral integrity and knowledgeable professionalism, must permeate everything that you do as a teacher. This chapter looks first at the idea of professionalism and its implications for personal conduct, then explores the bulleted statements in detail, showing how this part of the Standards relates to the eight standards set out in Part One of the Teachers' Standards.

The concept of professionalism

Teachers like to think of themselves as belonging to a profession, rather than pursuing a trade or doing a job. Jacques and Hyland (2007) describe professionals as exhibiting distinctive characteristics:

- possession of specialised knowledge and skills;

- the successful completion of specific education and training, with regular updating;

- adherence to a set of ethical standards when dealing with clients;

- a sense of responsibility for upholding the standards and reputation of the profession as a whole; and

- membership of an organisation which regulates admission to the profession and deals with issues of competence and conduct (Jacques and Hyland, 2007, p 202).

Each of these characteristics can be identified with respect to teaching, and you should have no difficulty in relating them to your own training and development as a teacher, except perhaps for the final statement, which continues to give rise to debate.

From 1998 to 2012 the professional body for teachers in England was the General Teaching Council for England (GTCE), established by parliament 'to contribute to improving standards of teaching and the quality of learning, and to maintain and improve standards of professional conduct among teachers, in the interests of the public' (DfEE, 1998). Parallel bodies were established for Wales and Northern Ireland, and some minor changes were made to the remit of the General Teaching Council for Scotland, which had already been in existence for some time. Following the change of Government in 2010 the incoming Education Secretary announced his intention to abolish the GTCE, which he claimed had done little to raise either standards or professionalism. Abolition took place in 2012, with responsibility for registration and regulation of teachers in England passing eventually to the National College for Teaching and Leadership (NCTL), an executive agency of the Department for Education. Opinion among teachers was divided, as the following comments demonstrate:

REFLECTIVE TASK

Reflecting on alternative viewpoints

Teacher A: *I could never see the point of the GTCE. We had to pay an annual fee of £36, but I couldn't see what I would get for this that I wouldn't be able to access from my union. Surely the Government should keep the register of teachers, and the school governors and local authorities should be responsible for disciplinary hearings.*

Teacher B: *I was sad to see the end of the GTCE. It was a chance for the teaching profession to show that it could regulate itself, rather than being dealt with by local councils and governments. Health service staff are registered and regulated by their own organisations such as the Nursing and Midwifery Council and the General Medical Council. I think the teaching profession should operate like that.*

» *With whom do you agree and why?*

It is worth noting that the Nursing and Midwifery Council was originally established by parliament, as recently as 2001, and is already perceived as independent of state control, so it will be interesting to see whether the NCTL develops in a similar way.

REFLECTIVE TASK

Reflecting on your reading

Read the following articles, which deal with the issue of teachers' professionalism, and consider the ways in which the perspectives portrayed by Kelly and Evans influence your own thinking about teaching as a profession.

Kelly, G (2011) Editorial – Few Mourned Passing of GTC, but There's a Gaping Hole Where Independent Regulator Should Be. *Times Educational Supplement,* 29 July 2011.

Kelly asserts that autonomy is a key feature of a profession and concludes that successful regulation has to be independent of government.

Evans, L (2011) The 'Shape' of Teacher Professionalism in England. *British Educational Research Journal,* 37 (5): 851–70.

Evans examines recent legislation (DfE, 2010) and questions whether – and to what extent – professionalism can be imposed by government reforms. Her analysis of the concept of professionalism leads her to claim that 'demanded' professionalism results in a lop-sided view of teaching by over-emphasising teachers' behaviours, to the exclusion of their attitudes and intellectual capacities.

Registering as a teacher

Currently, if you teach in England you will be registered with the NCTL. However, since education is a devolved responsibility within the United Kingdom, the arrangements are different in Scotland, Wales and Northern Ireland. All three have retained their General Teaching Councils (GTCs), with which you will have to be registered if you teach in their areas. If you wish to move between countries in the United Kingdom you will need to register with the appropriate body. The NCTL and the GTCs are responsible for setting and monitoring the standards for registration in the four countries of the United Kingdom, and you need to be aware that there are some differences from one country to another in requirements regarding academic qualifications. The details of these bodies, their professional standards and other requirements for registration are readily accessed by means of their websites.

Your contract of employment

In schools in England and Wales which are maintained by local authorities, teachers' contracts are based on the *School Teachers' Pay and Conditions* document (DfE, 2013a), known as the Blue Book, which is updated annually. Schools are required to implement these regulations, which deal with what you are required to do as a teacher and with salary scales.

Government reforms to these matters can be traced through successive versions of the Blue Book, and sometimes give rise to disputes between government and teaching unions. Another document, *The Conditions of Service for Schoolteachers in England and Wales* (LGA, 2000), known as the Burgundy Book, deals with other, non-statutory conditions of service, agreed between the teaching unions and the local authority employers. Local authorities accept these conditions as binding.

Maintained schools include:

* Community Schools (formerly County Schools);

* Voluntary Controlled Schools (mostly Church Schools, where the Local Authority is the employer but the governors may make conditions related to the school's religious character);

* Voluntary Aided Schools (mostly of a religious character, where the governing body as the employer may make conditions including reference to candidates' religious commitment);

* Foundation Schools, where the governing body is the employer; and

* Trust Schools, state-funded schools which receive extra support (usually non-monetary) from a charitable trust made up of partners working together for the benefit of the school.

Note that not all schools (including independent and private schools, academies and free schools) are bound by the Burgundy Book, although some choose to use it. They may therefore have different arrangements for, and expectations of, their staff. Check carefully before signing a contract, and take appropriate advice, for example from a union or professional association. Find out whether work in a school to which you apply for a post will count towards the induction period (normally, one year's satisfactory full-time work or its part-time equivalent) required before final accreditation as a fully qualified teacher.

Professional conduct

Central to your work as a teacher is your responsibility towards the children you teach, not only for their progress in the curriculum but also for their personal development and their general well-being. The expectations set out in Part Two of the Teachers' Standards encapsulate the key characteristics of a professional relationship between teachers and pupils, as well as expressing specific requirements about safeguarding children. They also demonstrate how teachers should relate to the ethos of the schools in which they teach and to the culture, traditions and values of Britain. Each of these merits separate consideration.

Relating to pupils

Several of the Standards convey implications about your relationship to the children you teach. They ask you to set them a positive example in attitudes, values and behaviour (Chapter 1), guide and encourage them (Chapter 2), promote their intellectual curiosity and foster a love of learning (Chapter 4), demonstrate an understanding of their developmental needs (Chapter 5), give them constructive feedback (Chapter 6) and manage their behaviour effectively (Chapter 7). These expectations are summed up in one of the exemplification statements in Part Two of the Teachers' Standards: 'treating pupils with dignity, building relationships rooted in mutual respect, and at all times observing proper boundaries appropriate to a teacher's professional position'. If you ask adults to recall teachers from their own schooldays, it is usually aspects of their overall demeanour that they remember, rather than the subject matter that they learned from them.

REFLECTIVE TASK

Reflecting on alternative viewpoints

Consider the following reflections:

Parent A: *One teacher, Mr X, was too friendly and tried to make out that he was one of us. As a result he couldn't control the class and there was often general mayhem in his lessons.*

Parent B: *On the other hand, Mrs Y went too far in the other direction. She was so strict that we were afraid of her, and it tended to put you off her lessons.*

Parent C: *Yes, and she could be really sarcastic, which I thought was terrible in a teacher.*

Parent D: *Do you remember Miss W, who taught the top juniors? She was five foot nothing, and some of the children were taller than she was. I never heard her shout, but she could keep order. I don't know how she did it, but you just wouldn't want to play her up.*

Parent C: *She could take a joke, too, and we had a lot of fun in her class. But when she said, 'it's time to get down to work', we knew we had to get on with it.*

Those recollections, from a cross-section of parents at a school reunion, are probably typical, and they are more than merely anecdotal. When the Hay/McBer organisation was commissioned by the government to undertake research into teacher effectiveness (see Chapter 1), one of their findings was that the pupils' opinions of their teachers mattered greatly when judging the effectiveness of their lessons.

Importantly, Hay/McBer concluded that there was no one approach which guaranteed uniquely high outcomes. Teachers with a wide variety of qualities and characteristics can be effective. 'Teachers are not clones' is one of the sub-headings in their report (Hay/McBer, 2000, para 1.1.14).

Hay/McBer's work has informed the compilation of standards for teachers since the beginning of the century, and consequently the expectations about 'treating pupils with dignity, building relationships rooted in mutual respect, and at all times observing proper boundaries appropriate to a teacher's professional position' are in part based upon what pupils told the researchers, and thus offer something of an evidence base for the standards.

Safeguarding and protecting children

The term 'safeguarding' refers broadly to an approach which ensures that children grow up in circumstances consistent with the provision of safe and effective care, so that they have the best chances in life. 'Child Protection' is a particular instance of safeguarding referring to the activity undertaken to protect specific children who are suffering, or are likely to suffer, significant harm (DfE 2013b, p 85). Periodic failures in child protection receive extended media attention, whereas the many successful interventions are hidden from public view. As a professional in teaching, you have a responsibility to be vigilant about your pupils' well-being with regard to both child protection and the broader matter of safeguarding. Your general duty of safeguarding is dealt with in Chapter 1 (A Safe and Stimulating Classroom). The more specific matter of Child Protection merits its own section.

Child protection

> Shockingly, some children are at risk from the very people they should be able to rely on for love and care. We all have a responsibility to do everything possible to protect these vulnerable children.
>
> (DfES, 2009)

This quotation introduces the government's response to two reports by Lord Laming (Laming, 2003 and Laming, 2009) following the death of Victoria Climbié, an incident which gave rise to much public debate and political action designed to protect children from abuse. Because school staff members have regular contact with children, they are likely to be in a position to notice signs that all is not well. If you have concerns about a child in school, you have a duty to take action.

Macpherson (2011, p 138) draws attention to a mass of legislation and statutory guidance, from 1989 onwards, covering the right of children to protection from harm, arrangements to prevent would-be abusers from being appointed to posts in school and requirements for multi-professional working. With respect to schools, all members of staff are required to attend training in safeguarding and child protection at regular intervals, and every school's policy and practice in safeguarding children is closely examined during Ofsted inspections. Despite the thoroughness of these arrangements cases of serious abuse, sometimes resulting in death, continue to come to light periodically and give rise to calls for further public enquiries.

The Coalition government commissioned a review (Munro, 2011) into all aspects of child protection. Its headline conclusion was summarised as follows in a report by the UK parliament's Education Committee:

> The system had become overly prescriptive and bureaucratic and the balance between prescription and the exercise of professional judgement needed to be redressed so that "those working in child protection are able to stay child-centred.
>
> (House of Commons, 2012 p 8)

Munro calls for a move from a compliance to a learning culture, with professionals being given 'more scope to exercise professional judgement in deciding how best to help children and their families' (Munro, 2011, p 5). In other words, she had found that child protection practice relied too much on adhering to procedures and policies and too little on professionals noticing, recording and reporting concerns using their own judgement.

Munro's emphasis on the importance of remaining child-centred arises from instances of serious abuse in which professionals accepted the explanations and accounts of adults instead of following up on serious concerns about children.

REFLECTIVE TASK

Reflecting on alternative viewpoints

Reflect on the following contributions.

School Governor: *I recently attended a training session about governors' responsibilities for safeguarding and protecting children and was shocked by a case that we heard about. A child had regularly come to school with bad bruises, seemed to be losing weight over a period of time and appeared increasingly withdrawn. Whenever the head teacher raised it with the girl's mother there was always a plausible explanation: 'she tripped and hit her head', 'she fell down some steps', 'she's got a medical condition which affects her appetite', and so on. The girl died following a severe blow to the stomach, and it turned out that she'd been abused by her mother – physically beaten, deprived of food – for months. What's more, the mother was a lunchtime welfare assistant at the school.*

Course Tutor: *Professionals tend to be optimistic about people, and don't want to think ill of them. Unfortunately, in some of the worst cases of child abuse, the perpetrators are skilled at manipulating the situation and can systematically conceal the truth. Obviously, members of staff wouldn't expect that a colleague could ill-treat her child to the point of killing her, as in this instance. But however rare such a case may be, it shows that we need to be objective about the evidence before us, and to keep the child at the centre of our concerns.*

As you consider the case study referred to in the governor's contribution, reflect on your own reaction to the circumstances described.

» *How can you balance an expectation that adults will act responsibly towards all children with a disposition that is alert to the possibility that some will do the opposite?*

Every school must have a designated person, often the head teacher, with overall responsibility for safeguarding and child protection, and a nominated school governor to oversee policy and practice in these areas. Government guidance provides details of categories of abuse and neglect, and these offer insight into signs and behaviours that might indicate that a child is at risk (DfE, 2013b, p 85). If you are concerned about a child at school, whether from your observations, from what a child says or does, or from what someone else tells you, your duty of care in safeguarding and child protection requires you to act in three ways.

1.   Firstly, you must pay serious attention to the issue;

2.   Secondly, you should make a dated, signed written record of what you have seen, heard or read, keeping your notes objective;

3.   Thirdly, you must report your concerns to the school's designated teacher, giving them a copy of your written notes and keeping another copy in a secure place.

Normally, a professional's ethical duty towards clients (which includes children as well as parents and carers) includes a commitment to confidentiality, but suspected child abuse overrides that duty. No adverse consequences will befall you if you report such a concern, even if your fears eventually prove groundless, unless it could be shown that you were acting maliciously.

If a child discloses something to you that makes you concerned about their welfare, show them that you believe what they are saying and that it is not wrong for them to be telling you. Be very careful not to ask leading questions, as this may result in the child embroidering the truth, though it is appropriate to ask for clarification or to say, 'is there anything else you want to tell me?'

Investigations into child protection concerns are led by senior social workers, who draw together information from a range of disciplines, including health practitioners and the police as well as colleagues in social services. You may sometimes be asked to attend a case conference, but often the school's designated person does this, using your report as a key piece of information. Either way, your contribution will provide important knowledge about the child's circumstances and how they are being addressed.

The school context

Every school has its own distinctive ethos and a set of policies. These are overseen by the governing body, which is responsible for the overall direction of the school. The head teacher, as the person in charge of managing the school, is tasked with putting them into practice and has to report on them regularly to the governing body. Your professional responsibility is to have proper regard for the school's ethos and policies, and for the ways in which they are implemented.

School ethos

The concept of ethos deserves careful consideration. The Oxford Dictionary of English, 2003 defines it as 'the characteristic spirit of a culture, era or community as manifested in its attitudes and aspirations', noting its root in the Greek word ēthos, meaning 'nature or disposition'. One education authority, applying this to schools, states that

> *Ethos is the overall feeling and nature of a school. This includes the atmosphere in the school, relationships between pupils, staff, families and the wider community, the school building and grounds, the sense of welcome and positive learning in the classroom.*

> (Highland Council, 2010)

The fundamental point to note is that the ethos of an organisation such as a school depends on a set of beliefs and values. These may be set out in schools' mission or vision statements, though they often remain implicit, or only partially articulated. Consider the following examples of mission or vision statements from a range of schools:

REFLECTIVE TASK

Reflecting on your reading

»   *Identify the key values set out in the prospectuses of these four schools.*

»   *To which of them would you confidently send an application for a job?*

It is the aim of the school to develop the academic potential of each child, and to cater for the social, moral, physical and spiritual requirements of the individual in a happy and secure environment.

(W. Primary School)

Our Mission is to ensure a happy and secure learning environment where we celebrate the dignity and worth of all in our school community. As a Christian community we recognise that in loving others we love Jesus and so help each other to reach our full potential.

(St X's Roman Catholic Primary School)

The central aim of our school is to offer a friendly, positive, safe, caring and stimulating environment through trust and partnership between staff, pupils, parents, governors and links with the local community.

(Y. Primary School)

Z. is a welcoming, inclusive school, where everyone is valued in a safe, happy and healthy environment. Our school is a place of excellence, where learners thrive and succeed within a positive 'can-do' culture. We empower learners with the confidence to be independent and instil in them ambition and a life-long love of learning. As the learning hub of our diverse community, we welcome all members on our learning journey.

(Z. Primary School)

In addition to the overt religious convictions declared in St X's mission, a number of beliefs about education lurk beneath the surface of these statements. There are three main approaches to defining educational aims:

1.   One is about cultural transmission, emphasising transmission of knowledge from one generation to another, and is focused on curriculum content to be taught by teachers and learned by pupils;

2.   The second relates to the development of individuals, with a major concern for the fulfilment of their various potentials, and focuses on providing learners with a range of relevant experiences and equipping them to take every advantage of them;

3.   The third centres on the relationship between individuals and society, with a concern to make learners ready to play a full part in society, and it highlights skills for employability and social skills.

In the above examples you can trace elements of these three types of aim, with particular emphases apparent in each school.

A survey of educational legislation in England (Ewens, 2007) reveals the interweaving of the three types of aim, centred on the requirement dating from the 1944 Education Act that the education service should promote 'the spiritual, moral, mental and physical development of the community'. However, subsequently, especially since the mid-1980s, educational debate has largely been about the curriculum, to the exclusion of consideration of educational aims. This is unfortunate. After all, a curriculum is the vehicle by means of which aims can be realised. It is vital to have clear aims before designing a curriculum, otherwise you run the risk of saying, 'how do we get there?' without asking, 'where are we going?'

The Teachers' Standards require you to have a proper and professional regard for the ethos of your school. This does not compel you to commit yourself fully to the underpinning beliefs expressed. For example, you might be appointed to teach at St X's school without being a Roman Catholic, but you would have a duty to uphold the school's Christian foundation. Similarly, you would need to be able to give sympathetic support to the ethos statement of any school to which you were appointed. It is well worth reading and contemplating such statements before you apply for a post. After all, you will not wish to work in an environment whose main aims are in conflict with your deeply held views, any more than the head and governors will wish to appoint someone who finds it hard to give wholehearted support to their central vision. It is therefore a good idea to think clearly through your own views about the purposes of education, and to scrutinise the mission or vision statement of any school where you are thinking of applying for a post, to ensure as far as possible that there will be congruence between your values and those of the school.

REFLECTIVE TASK

Reflecting on your schooldays

»   *Looking back at your time at primary school what would you say, with hindsight, were the main aims of your school or schools?*

»   *How were these aims reflected in what you were taught and how the school was organised?*

»   *In what ways has your experience coloured your current ideas about the purposes of education?*

School policies and practice

School websites typically list a host of policies dealing with topics as diverse as the curriculum, behaviour, equal opportunities, special educational needs and healthy eating. The policies, adopted by the governing body, set out broad aims and principles. It is for the head teacher to lead the staff of the school in deciding how to implement these aspirations, using their best professional judgement. For example, an extract from School W's English policy states: 'Children should develop a clear and legible joined handwriting style, in order to promote effective written communication and self-expression'. The professional responsibility of the staff is to decide how this aspiration is to be achieved, by deciding for example how early children are to be taught to join letters, what particular style of joined writing is to be adopted and whether handwriting should be taught in dedicated handwriting sessions or during the course of lessons generally.

When you begin at a school as a teacher or trainee teacher you will have access to a staff handbook containing detailed guidance (masses of it) about every aspect of policy and practice. As part of your induction, the senior staff member responsible for your work will draw your attention to the most important procedures, but it will take you a considerable length of time to get to grips with the entirety of the school's agreed practices.

You have a professional responsibility to work within the policies and procedures adopted by the school. Usually this involves no more than adapting your planning and teaching to make them congruent with the arrangements set out in the staff handbook. Sometimes, however, it may mean that you find yourself expected to work in a way with which you disagree. For example, suppose you fundamentally disagree with the school's handwriting policy and practice, and prefer a completely different approach. It would be unprofessional in these circumstances to ignore the agreed policy and to substitute your own methods. Likewise, it would be improper to voice your opinions about this to your class or to parents at a parents' evening. It would, however, be entirely appropriate to mention your views to the head teacher or another senior colleague and to ask for the topic to be discussed at a staff meeting. Improvements in teaching and learning can often start with an informed debate in the staffroom, and you have every right to contribute your perspectives in a forum of your colleagues.

The Teachers' Standards emphasise the importance of maintaining high standards of attendance and punctuality, both because pupils can learn from your example and also because your presence is a crucial factor in the safe and efficient running of the school. Your school will have a set procedure for reporting absence because of illness or emergency, so that arrangements can be made for classes to be covered.

British values

The idea that education should include students' spiritual, moral, social and cultural values has long been an explicit aim in legislation in England, although the implications of this for teacher education and teachers' conduct have only occasionally been explicitly considered (Ewens, 1998, p 107f). Two bulleted points in Part Two of the Teachers' Standards seek to exemplify teachers' professional responsibility in this area:

- *showing tolerance of, and respect for the rights of others, and*
- *not undermining fundamental British values, including democracy, the rule of law, individual liberty and mutual respect, and tolerance of those with different faiths and beliefs.*

These requirements should be understood in the light of a long-held expectation that the education service should contribute to creating a coherent society. The term community cohesion came to prominence during the first decade of the twenty-first century (DCSF, 2007), as part of the government's response to disturbances in a number of major cities and concerns about a perceived rise in extreme political activity. The concept reflected a concern by government to build positive relationships among people from different groups and backgrounds, and to formulate and promote a set of values that would underpin a harmonious and diverse society. The same concerns, though arising from different circumstances, had motivated those who framed the 1944 Education Act, for whom the duty of fostering the spiritual and moral development of the community sprang from an aspiration to provide some of the 'glue' to hold society together when its unity was threatened at a time of war (Ewens, 1998, p 109).

REFLECTIVE TASK

Reflecting on your reading

DCSF (2007) offers a definition of community cohesion as part of its guidance to schools, and subsequent Ofsted inspections included a focus on the extent to which schools were actively promoting community cohesion.

Phillips et al. (2011) provide a comprehensive review of the progress made by schools in response to the requirement to promote community cohesion and PREVENT (a scheme to prevent violent extremism).

Shepherd (2010b) records the contrasting responses of two politicians to the news that Ofsted would cease to inspect schools' work in community cohesion. One regretted the move because 'an emphasis on community cohesion in schools enables pupils to understand the differences between cultures and backgrounds', whereas the other welcomed it, claiming that 'the best contribution to community cohesion a school can make is providing a good education for all its children'.

» *After reading these texts, reflect on your response to the views of the two politicians cited by Shepherd. To what extent do you agree with either of them?*

Since the vast majority of children in Britain spend significant periods of time in the school system, it is not surprising that expectations are placed on teachers to contribute to fostering community cohesion.

Examples in Chapters 3, 4 and 7 illustrate how you can use your knowledge of the curriculum, lesson planning and behaviour management to give children insight into, and experience of, concepts such as democracy, the rule of law, individual liberty and mutual respect, and tolerance of people with different faiths and beliefs. As a professional, your words and actions ought to complement your teaching.

One issue confronting teachers is the extent to which it is appropriate for them to express their personal opinions about matters of belief, for example regarding political, moral or religious issues. If you remain silent on such matters you could give an impression that they are not important. On some issues, for example racist comments and actions, it is imperative that you speak up, but on others, where a diverse range of lawful opinions is held in society, if you reveal your own views you might risk over-influencing children's ideas and attitudes. Teachers' utterances often carry great weight, especially with younger pupils, and it is vital not to take advantage of their vulnerability by pressing your viewpoints inappropriately.

REFLECTIVE TASK

Reflecting on alternative viewpoints

Consider these comments from two head teachers to assist your reflection.

Head teacher 1: *Our school vision statement makes it clear that our work is based on a code of ethical principles. We drew up a set of values that we believe should underpin the life of the school. These were agreed by the governors and staff, shared with the PTA [Parent–Teacher Association] committee and published on our website. I would expect teachers to speak and act in line with this code, so that there is a consistent example for the children.*

Head teacher 2: *We discussed at a staff meeting how members of staff ought to deal with children's questions about potentially controversial topics. We agreed that it is usually right to give a straightforward answer, pitched appropriately to the age of the child. However, we decided to make a habit of suggesting that children put the same question to other adults, at school and at home. One teacher reported an occasion when she had given an answer to a child's question about a religious issue, and had then invited the teaching assistant to give her view, which she knew was different from her own. We discussed this, and concluded that it was invaluable for children to learn that people could disagree sincerely about something without falling out about it.*

» *What, in your view, is an appropriate way for teachers to respond to children's questions about their personal beliefs and opinions?*

Teachers and members of other professions are commonly expected to demonstrate a higher than average level of personal integrity. Irrespective of whether you find that just or fair, it is an expectation which is clearly conveyed in Part Two of the Teachers' Standards, and thus forms part of the definition of your professional identity and accountability.

Performance of understanding

Thinking about the school in which you work or have recently worked, respond to the prompts after each intended learning outcome, as a means of identifying your knowledge and understanding of the issues covered in the chapter.

- *an appreciation of the concept of a profession and what makes teaching a profession;*
  - Identify from the school's staff handbook examples of teachers' duties or responsibilities that illustrate the professional characteristics set out by Jacques and Hyland (2007, p 202).
  - Explain your understanding of what makes teaching a profession.
- *some insights into the relationship between personal conduct and professional responsibility;*
  - Locate in your recent work some examples demonstrating how you used your personal judgement to ensure that you fulfilled a professional responsibility.
  - In what ways have you responded to the requirement to support the ethos of the school?
  - Define what you believe to be the ideal relationship between a teacher and the class. How do you go about creating and sustaining that type of rapport with your class?
- *knowledge of professional and legal frameworks within which teachers operate;*
  - Find in the staff handbook the information that tells you what to do if you become seriously concerned about a child's safety and welfare. Rehearse in your mind the steps that you would take.
  - What guidance does the staff handbook offer to ensure that you deal with pupils' behaviour lawfully?
- *your awareness of the professional knowledge, understanding, skills and attitudes which teachers must display.*
  - Identify a few examples of ways in which your practice has been enhanced as a result of your reading or participation in some training.
  - Articulate your strategies for dealing with children's questions about your beliefs and opinions, if possible identifying an example and evaluating your handling of it.

Taking it further

Evans, L (2008) Professionalism, Professionality and the Development of Education Professionals. *British Journal of Education Studies*, 56 (1): 20–38.

Laming, H (2009) *The Protection of Children in England: A Progress Report*. HC 330. London: The Stationery Office.

Swann, M et al. (2010) Teachers' Conceptions of Teacher Professionalism in England in 2003 and 2006. *British Educational Research Journal*, 36 (4): 549–71.

References

Department for Children, Schools and Families (DCSF) (2007) *Guidance on the Duty to Promote Community Cohesion*. London: DCSF.

Department for Education (2010) *The Importance of Teaching: The Schools White Paper 2010*. Cm 7980. London: The Stationary Office.

Department for Education (DfE) (2013a) *The School Teachers' Pay and Conditions Document*. London: DfE.

Department for Education (DfE) (2013b) *Working Together to Safeguard Children*. London: DfE.

Department for Education and Employment (DfEE) (1998) *Teaching and Higher Education Act 1998. [c.30]*. London: DfEE.

Department for Education and Skills (DfES) (2009) *The Protection of Children in England: Action Plan – the Government's Response to Lord Laming*. Cm 7589. London: DfES.

Evans, L (2011) The 'Shape' of Teacher Professionalism in England. *British Educational Research Journal*, 37 (5): 851–70.

Ewens, T (1998) Teacher Education and Personal, Spiritual, Moral, Social and Cultural Education, in Richards, C, Simco, N and Twiselton, S (eds) *Primary Teacher Education: High Status? High Standards?* London: Falmer Press.

Ewens, T (2007) Spiritual, Moral, Social and Cultural Values in the Classroom, in Jacques, K and Hyland, R (eds) *Professional Studies: Primary and Early Years.* Third edition. Exeter: Learning Matters.

Hay/McBer Group (2000) *Research into Teacher Effectiveness: A Model of Teacher Effectiveness.* (DfEE Research Report 216). London: DfEE.

Highland Council (2010) *Learning and Teaching Toolkit: Ethos.* Available online at www.highland. gov.uk/learninghere/supportforschoolstaff/ltt/issuepapers/ethos (accessed 26 September 2013).

House of Commons (2012) *Children First: The Child Protection System in England*. HC137. London: The Stationery Office.

Jacques, K and Hyland, R (eds) (2007) *Professional Studies: Primary and Early Years.* Third edition. Exeter: Learning Matters.

Kelly, G (2011) Editorial – Few Mourned Passing of GTC, but There's a Gaping Hole Where Independent Regulator Should Be. *Times Educational Supplement,* 29 July 2011.

Laming, H (2003) *The Victoria Climbié Inquiry: Report of an Inquiry by Lord Laming.* Cm 5730. London: The Stationery Office.

Local Government Association (LGA) et al. (2000) *The Conditions of Service for Schoolteachers in England and Wales*. London: LGA.

Macpherson, P (2011) Safeguarding Children, in Hansen, A (ed) *Primary Professional Studies*. Exeter: Learning Matters.

Munro, E (2011) *The Munro Review of Child Protection; Final Report: A Child Centred System*. Cm 8062. London: The Stationery Office.

Phillips, C, Tse, D and Johnson, F (2011) *Community Cohesion and Prevent: How Have Schools Responded?* DFE Research Report 085. London: DfE.

Shepherd, J (2010a) 'Deeply Sceptical' Michael Gove Calls Time on Teaching Watchdog. *The Guardian,* 3 June 2010.

Shepherd, J (2010b) Community Cohesion Slips off Ofsted's Agenda. *The Guardian,* 20 October 2010.

The General Teaching Council for Northern Ireland www.gtcni.org.uk

The General Teaching Council for Scotland www.gtcs.org.uk

The General Teaching Council for Wales www.gtcw.org.uk

The National College for Teaching and Leadership www.nationalcollege.org.uk

Postscript: reflecting on the Standards

The nine chapters that make up this book are designed to promote a reflective approach to becoming and continuing as a primary school teacher. They are designed to ensure that you have given due attention to each of the Teachers' Standards, and have thought about a range of factors and contested ideas which comprise current educational debate. The exercises entitled 'Performance of understanding' are organised to allow you to articulate evidence that you meet the Standards. However, one important topic remains. The purpose of this postscript is to draw attention to some key issues that are not addressed by the Standards, but which are crucial to a serious discussion about a teacher's professional role and duties.

What are the aims of education?

The Teachers' Standards are silent about the long-term goals of education. The preamble to the Standards states that 'teachers make the education of their pupils their first concern, and are accountable for achieving the highest possible standards in work and conduct'. You might regard this as so obvious as to be a truism. Trace the outworking of that statement through the Standards, however, and you will conclude that they portray a very restricted view of the purposes of education. Apart from the first bulleted point in Standard 8 – 'make a positive contribution to the wider life and ethos of the school' – the Standards are confined to statements about the teaching and learning of the formal curriculum. It is true that the issue of pupils' behaviour is highlighted, but here too the emphasis is on managing behaviour so that pupils can make the best possible progress in the curriculum.

Good behaviour and good progress in the curriculum are, of course, to be prized and promoted, but surely education is about that and far more besides. Traditionally, and in law, the English education system has had a duty to promote pupils' spiritual, moral, mental and physical development (DES, 1944), and their social and cultural development as well (DES, 1988). The notion that education should be about the formation of rounded persons is pervasive in the independent sector, and implicit in much of the discourse of teachers, parents and governors in the public sector. But this has been overlooked in the Teachers' Standards.

A main reason for separating the broader aims of education from the specific ones associated with learning the formal curriculum relates to the measurability of progress. Governments and Ofsted have focused increasingly on those aspects of education that can conveniently be measured mathematically, and this has been to the detriment of others that are not easily quantified. The Confederation of British Industry (CBI) report (CBI, 2012) reasserts the importance of a broad education by pointing out that inculcating a wide range of personal qualities is crucial to equipping young people to play a full part in a rapidly changing society. You might well think that the Standards should more adequately reflect this aspiration.

Educating for an unknown future

It has always been a function of the education service to respond to the needs of society. One obvious aspect relates to school leavers' employability. Another, equally important, concerns preparing young people for other roles in adult life, including making and sustaining relationships, parenthood, managing household finances and generally making their way in the world.

Hayes (2006) offers a useful reminder that education for all is a very recent notion. From around 1770 it was provided patchily by voluntary movements, especially the churches, and only from 1870 by the state, which filled the gaps where there were no voluntary schools. Its development can be linked to a growing need for a trained or educated workforce. For a time it was acceptable to have an elite with a broad, liberal education, while the mass of the population learned just the three Rs. Later, around a quarter of pupils were deemed fit for an academic grammar school education and destined for the professions, while the rest received a curriculum with a vocational focus. Now, the increasing complexity of the workplace, the rapidity of technological change and the unknown nature of future occupations mean that a rounded education is needed by all. Since new knowledge is created every day, it is also a requirement that pupils should learn how to learn, and how to find and create new applications for their knowledge. Pring's (1996) attempt to synthesise the best of the old liberal tradition of education with the benefits of a vocational curriculum may look like a compromise, but it may be an idea whose time has come.

What teachers need to know and profess

The somewhat instrumental view of the nature of teaching displayed in the Standards is at odds with Richards' claim that the teacher is 'a frighteningly significant person whose teaching helps to shape attitudes to learning at a most sensitive time in children's development' (Richards, 2009, p 20). Richards' view indicates that it is not only your knowledge, but also your values and attitudes, that you communicate to your pupils, so you need to think carefully about what you are portraying to your class.

That does not mean that your values and attitudes should be suppressed in the classroom, since a broad and balanced education must include consideration of values, beliefs and attitudes alongside the learning of facts, skills and concepts.

Michel de Montaigne (1533–1592) was a French statesman, soldier, philosopher and essayist. Two of his essays, 'On Schoolmasters' Learning' and 'On Educating Children', are classic texts well worth reading in Screech's recent English translation, as they explore ideas that continually recur in debates about education. Commenting on education in his day, he complains that

> From the way we have been taught, it is no wonder that neither master nor pupils become more able, even though they do know more. In truth the care and fees of our parents aim only at furnishing our heads with knowledge: nobody talks about judgement or virtue...We readily inquire, 'Does he know Greek or Latin?' 'Can he write poetry or prose?' But what matters most is what we put last: 'Has he become better or wiser?' We ought to find out not who understands most but who understands best. We work merely to fill the memory, leaving the understanding and the sense of right and wrong empty. Just as birds sometimes go in search of grain, carrying it in their beaks without tasting it to stuff it down the beaks of their young, so too do our schoolmasters go foraging for learning in their books and merely lodge it on the tips of their lips, only to spew it out and scatter it on the wind.
>
> (Montaigne, 2003, p 154)

Montaigne would have recognised the English education system in the twenty-first century as exhibiting at least some of the characteristics of the French one that he commented on in the sixteenth. His critique carries with it the implications that children need not only knowledge, but also well-developed faculties of wisdom, judgement and moral values so that they know how to use their learning aright. His conclusions are similar to those of Whitehead (1950, p 6) in his claim that 'education is the acquisition of the art of the utilisation of knowledge'.

If Montaigne is right, as I believe he is, it means that teachers such as you and I need to be able to display far more than the qualities required to say that we have 'met the Standards'. But the Standards are, at least, a start.

References

CBI (The Confederation of British Industry) (2012) *First Steps: A New Approach for our Schools*. London: CBI.

Department of Education and Science (DES) (1944) *Education Act, 1944*. London: HMSO.

Department of Education and Science (DES) (1988) *The Education Reform Act, 1988*. London: DES.

Hayes, D (2006) Schools and Classrooms, in Sharp, J, Ward, S and Hankin, L, *Education Studies: An Issues-Based Approach*. Exeter: Learning Matters.

Montaigne, M de (2003) 'On Schoolmasters' Learning' and 'On Educating Children'. *The Complete Essays*. Translated by M A Screech. Third edition. London: Penguin Press.

Pring, R (1996) Values and Education Policy, in Halstead, J M and Taylor, M J (eds) *Values in Education and Education in Values*. London: Falmer Press.

Richards, C (2009) Primary Teaching: A Personal Perspective, in Arthur, J, Grainger, T and Wray, D (eds) *Learning to Teach in the Primary School*. Abingdon: Routledge.

Whitehead, A N (1950) The Aims of Education, in *The Aims of Education and Other Essays*. Second edition. London: Ernest Benn.

Index

Notes and reflections